Who Gets the
Yellow Bananas?

Who Gets the Yellow Bananas?

*Wry New England Thoughts
on the Human Condition*

by Joann Snow Duncanson

Edited by Frederick Samuels, Ph.D.

Peter E. Randall Publisher
Portsmouth, NH · 2000

Peter E. Randall Publisher
Box 4726, Portsmouth, NH 03802-4726

Distributed by University Press of New England,
    Hanover and London

Designed by Tom Allen, Pear Graphic Design
Cover illustration by Bob Nilson
Photos on p. vii and p. 60, Joe Shamy

Library of Congress Cataloging-in-Publication Data

Duncanson, Joann Snow
    Who gets the yellow bananas? : wry New England thoughts
on human condition / by Joann Snow Duncanson ; edited by
Frederick Samuels.
    p. cm.
    ISBN 0-914339-83-4 (alk. paper)
    1. American wit and humor. I. Samuels, Frederick. II. Title.

PN6162 .D845 2000

814'.54--dc21

                                        99-087047

In dedication . . .

. . . to my children, Heidi and Scott, who always responded graciously to a mother who occasionally let her imagination run away with her;

. . . to the faithful readers of my columns, who so often thanked me for seeing the world through Bombeck-colored glasses;

and finally,
. . . to Fred Samuels, for inspiring me in so many ways, not the least of which was convincing me that this book would come to be.

Contents

Foreword

THE essays in this book are all by the award-winning columnist, Joann Snow Duncanson. They have been selected by her from among those published in the *Peterborough Transcript*, the *Portsmouth Herald,* and the *Middlesex News* of Framingham, Massachusetts. Several were also aired on New Hampshire Public Radio.

I have simply arranged the essays into sections. Any annotation of the essays would, I believe, be superfluous; they speak for themselves. It was a distinct pleasure for me to work with these essays. This writer deserves to be read and recognized as both a down-to-earth humorist and a compassionate observer of the human condition.

—Frederick Samuels, Ph.D.

Before you begin . . .

THIS book is not about fruit. It's about being able to look at the situations in which we find ourselves, and laugh. For instance, "Who Gets the Yellow Bananas?", my first story in the book, deals with being in the right place at the right time in life. How is it, we ask, that for a precious few shoppers, the bananas are always a perfect yellow, while when you and I cruise into the produce department they are either green or just one step ahead of banana heaven? Then we laugh, reminding ourselves that, indeed, life isn't always fair—especially at the banana counter.

These pages also feature vignettes of ordinary people: Mildred McLaughlin and her rose garden; Mrs. Kosberg and her lingerie shop; Phil Levine and his gas station. Also on these pages you will find me pulling back the curtain on my own family's life so that you can look inside and laugh or cry with me, according to the situation.

So, whether you purchased this book when it was still warm from the printer or you discovered it years later on some dusty, used book shelf, I hope that after reading it you will decide you were in the right place at the right time to do so. In other words, you are indeed someone who gets the yellow bananas.

—*Joann Snow Duncanson*

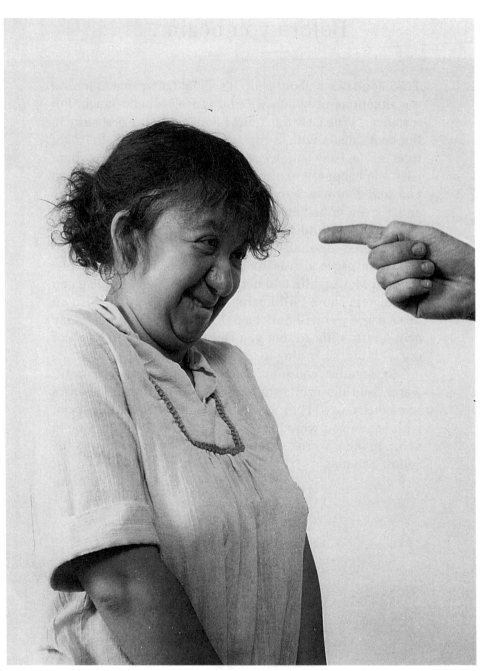

Photo: Joe Shamy

I. Laughing at Ourselves

Humor
  is healthful
    better than grief
      better than despair
Humor
  is nothing to laugh at!

—*Frederick Samuels*

Who gets the yellow bananas?

WHILE the world struggles with ponderous issues of great magnitude, I admit to sometimes directing my attention to matters of less global consequence—such as, who gets the yellow bananas?

Surely one of the most perplexing mysteries known to the modern shopper is why, whenever we go to the supermarket to buy bananas, they are not yellow but green. And not just one of them is green, you will notice; they are ALL green. Either that, or they are geriatric and have turned brown and spotted, and are one step away from banana heaven.

I never seem to hit it right when it comes to finding ready-to-eat bananas. I know that I am supposed to buy them when they are green, and while they are ripening, eat the green ones I got last week which in theory would have turned yellow by now. This is all well and good, but bananas have minds of their own. I can leave the house in the morning knowing they are beginning to turn yellow, then come home at night to find that they've put themselves on *fast forward*, are covered with brown spots and are beyond salvation . . . and I throw them out.

So who gets the yellow bananas, anyway?

It must all come down to the old saying about being in the right place at the right time. Some of us spend our whole lives just missing the mark. When we finally get to the cash register in the checkout line the "Closed" sign goes up. We could sit at a Las Vegas one-armed bandit machine for hours and lose our shirts, but the minute we move to the next machine, someone who just got off the bus from Peoria can sit down at our old one, put in the first quarter and suddenly bells and whistles go off and the money comes tumbling out.

I've never been in the right place at the right time when it comes to fashion either. When I was my thinnest, the huge tent dresses were in, and when I was in my prime pre-cellulite years, gawky Bermuda shorts replaced short shorts, covering up any attributes I thought I had.

I was carrying children and burping babies during the '60's when the mini skirts were in. Then by the time they came back in again, my legs had developed fat knees and spider veins.

One day over lunch, my friend Sister Theresa Marie and I were discussing this business of how important it is to be in the right place at the right time and she shared some of her experiences with me. I should interject here that Sister TM is not what most of us think of as a typical nun. She is a little off the beaten path.

Sister Theresa Marie is a poet, and the first time I ever saw her she was doing a poetry reading in a little storefront coffee house on a city's back street. She shared the spotlight with a young man from Maine who played guitar. They met by being in the right place at the right time—sitting next to each other on a Greyhound bus. She introduced herself as a poet and he to her as a musician. It wasn't until later that he discovered she was a nun and she learned he was a plumber by trade. She began sending him her poetry and he commenced setting it to music. The result of their melded talents was most evident that night in the coffee house.

But Sister TM told me that sometimes even the religious are not in the right place at the right time.

Once, she said, her convent was located in the heart of the city near many cultural activities she wanted to attend. However, since the laws of her order dictated that she could not go out alone, she always had to scurry around to find another nun to go with her—or stay home. And she often had to stay home. She was in the right place, but at the wrong time.

Today, many of the old bans have been lifted, (her habit, for instance, has long since been cut up into little pieces), the convent has relocated so far out in the country that though she has the freedom to attend functions alone, she complains, "you can't get there from here"! So with 20 nuns taking turns with the one vehicle, she's decided that now she's in the wrong place even though it's the right time.

I told her I fully understood her plight because that's how it is with me and bananas.

Perhaps there should be a school for people like us. A place where we can hone our lucky streaks or learn to recalibrate our timing mechanisms so our lives will be filled with good fortune and our shopping carts will overflow with perfect, potassium-filled yellow bananas.

We should live so long.

Erma Bombeck, where are you?

I STILL miss Erma Bombeck. It was sad to see her go, especially since her mind didn't seem quite ready to sit down yet; her wits were still up and running, razor sharp and facile. She was still throwing out zany but often pithy commentaries on situations which the reader not only recognized, but *lived* day by day. The problem was that her body didn't keep up with that mind of hers. Kidneys failed, a breast went wrong, and death finally told her she'd had her last laugh.

That's the whole secret, isn't it—having our minds and bodies come out even? Yet it seems that often either our faculties are very much intact but our livers give out, or our minds quit even though we can still run a pretty decent mile.

There are exceptions, of course, like my friend Thelma. Thelma is a delightful woman who chronologically is in her 95th year, a fact which seems to have no bearing on how she looks or acts. For instance, at her weekly bowling league she not only keeps score for the whole crew, but sometimes out-bowls the others, some of whom are thirty years her junior. Thelma also plays the piano "for the old folks" in rest homes, and wouldn't think of leaving the house until her nails are perfectly manicured and her outfit coordinated. She has that rare combination of mind and body coming out even.

Erma Bombeck, however, wasn't so lucky—her clock didn't run as long as Thelma's. Everyone says that if it were possible, she probably would have had a funny slant on even her own death because that's how she was.

As Erma herself could attest, humor isn't something you can shut off too easily; it's always there just under the surface ready to bubble up. That's how it was with her. How else could she have turned out those columns twice a week for over 25 years?

Anyone who wrote books with titles like, *If Life is a Bowl of Cherries—What Am I doing in the Pits?* and *The Grass is Always Greener Over the Septic Tank* had to be inately funny.

Every so often a reader refers to me as a New England version of Erma Bombeck. Except for the fact that she is deceased, I take this is as a distinct compliment. To have something in common with a wit such as Erma had is definitely flattering.

Erma would probably agree with me, however, when I say that being funny isn't always a gift. I learned early on that having a keen sense of humor can sometimes be a curse. The night of my senior prom was a case in point. (How can she STILL remember THAT, you ask? Easy! We don't tend to forget sheer humiliation!)

On that fateful night, four of us double-dated at the event which mandated that no self respecting teenager would come home before dawn. Otherwise, it would look as if: (a) we didn't have a good time; (b) we were wimps; or (c) both. Since this date wasn't a match made in heaven, we filled the hours between the prom and going home by driving around the countryside.

To help pass the time, I began to tell funny stories and one-liners over which the couple in the back seat would convulse in laughter. My date, however, was not so amused. In fact, at some point when we were out on some gawd-forsaken road to who-knows-where, he pulled the car over and said, "If you are going to be funnier than I am, you can walk home." Now I was a good walker but not THAT good, so I never said a funny word the rest of that night.

I learned a life-long lesson that night; while most women don't seem to mind if another woman is faster with a one-liner than she, many men prefer to think we women are a little slower on the humor uptake. So, as I say, being funny isn't always a blessing.

On the plus side, laughter has certainly kept some of us off the psychiatrist's couch. Erma's writing did that for us. For the few moments it took us to read her columns, we could relax, forget our troubles, sometimes even let loose a belly laugh, and just plain feel better at the end of it all. Without a single medical degree, she administered blood pressure medicine, column by column.

One of my favorite Bombeck subjects was child rearing. In *Motherhood: The Second Oldest Profession*, she dealt with that perfect creature called "everybody else's mother" You know, the one your children would refer to whenever you tried to hand down a little discipline. Said Erma, "Everybody else's mother is right out of the pages of Greek mythology—mysterious, obscure, and surrounded by hearsay. She eats jellybeans for breakfast, drinks milk out of a carton, sleeps late, smokes and grinds the ashes into the carpet with her toe . . . and she has never used the word No."

Throughout her career, Erma had her share of skeptics—those who regarded her as a lightweight, a mere blip on the publishing screen. Well, for a lightweight she certainly knew how to parley a sense of humor and marketing know-how with a laser sharp insight into human nature. Twelve honorary doctorate degrees later she was laughing all the way to the bank, and in the process she made deposits in our own mental health accounts which continue to gain interest for us today.

I still miss Erma Bombeck.

We're letting it all hang out

I'M NOT sure, but I think we made a little bit of history at our condominium association's annual meeting the other night. At least, that's the way it seems to me.

Anything can happen when we get condominium dwellers together in a forum where they can speak their minds about things they never had to consider when they lived in free-standing houses. Who's running the water late at night, for instance, or whose stereo is too loud. From plumbing to personality conflicts, we've handled them all. Luckily we're a pretty congenial group and enjoy our small, unique neighborhood.

At this year's annual meeting, everyone was in an especially good mood. We were in agreement with the financial report, and even approved the budget without too much moaning and groaning. And, for the first time in years, the maintenance report was a positive one, since Jon Nichols and his painting crew had just finished giving the entire place a fresh, new look. Then finally, our new officers were voted in.

Just as we were about to adjourn, however, the new owner in Unit #8 straightened up in her chair, cleared her throat and said quietly, "Excuse me—I have a request. I wonder, since my unit is way in the back, if I could possibly put up a clothesline."

Silence.

She persevered. "I've always hung out my laundry, and I thought if I got one of those circular, collapsible clotheslines and took it in when it's not in use, it might be all right. I'd be discreet about it. I'd never hang anything out on Sundays or holidays."

Then she sat back and waited for the reply she feared the most. And it came.

"Clotheslines aren't allowed in a condominium," the other owners chorused. "It says so right in the bylaws: *No clothing, laundry, rugs or other objects shall be hung, shaken or thrown from any window or exterior portions of a unit or otherwise left placed in such a way as to be exposed to public view.*"

If you've ever lived in a condominium you know that the bylaws can be both a curse and a blessing. They may prevent you from parking your beloved camper in your driveway, but on the other hand, if your neighbor starts cluttering up his front yard with pink flamingos, you have somewhere to turn. Fortunately our complex is small—only 11 units—but that doesn't mean we don't all have different opinions on things. Like the clotheslines.

After that quotation about "hanging, shaking and throwing things in such a way to be exposed to public view," I figured the subject of clotheslines was dead in the water, but not so.

Suddenly a discussion started up about clotheslines and why they have disappeared from the American scene. We began to grow nostalgic about clotheslines we all knew and loved and how some of the best neighborhood conversations in our mothers' times as well as ours, took place while hanging out the wash.

We got all but teary-eyed when we reminisced about getting into bed at night between sheets fresh from the line, with that indescribable aroma yet to be duplicated by modern science. We suddenly realized that most of us represented the last generation to know what that was like. The advent of electric dryers brought us a sense of liberation, yet even with all their perfumed softeners thrown in, they can't begin to manufacture that fresh-air scent.

We began questioning a society that would look upon clean clothes hanging on a line as somehow unsightly or offensive.

"What crime would it be, anyway?" one of the owners asked.

That's when it happened. For the first time in the five

years we've been in existence, the Garden Homes Condominium Association voted to override a bylaw. We decided the time had come for us to say it's okay to hang clean clothes out on a line.

Oh sure, there will undoubtedly be some restrictions about what they look like and where they are placed—and even how long clothes can be left on them—but at least they will be allowed.

I don't think our Unit #8 lady could believe her ears when the vote was taken. She probably went home that night in shock.

The next morning a young mother from Unit #3 rushed over to ask if it was true that she could actually hang wash outside now. When I told her it was, her face lit up. "Finally, I can hang out the cloth diapers!" She wasted no time. Later that day I noticed that she'd strung a line to a tree and there flapping in the sunlight were the dancing diapers. They were a beautiful sight.

I assume that by now the lady in #8 has already gone to the hardware store to get her rotating, collapsible model clothesline. The rest of us will hang things out as the spirit moves us and we'll trust that the other neighbors on the street will regard this not as an eyesore but as a wholesome state-ment of cleanliness. A mini-rebellion against today's gallop-ing technology and rising energy costs, flapping in the sunny breeze.

So that's the history-making news from the condos. Clotheslines are back and long may they wave. By the way, tonight when you climb into a bed made up with linens from the dryer, you can think of us over here at the Garden Homes (especially our lady in #8) sleeping soundly between some of the freshest smelling sheets in town.

And now for our speaker,
what's-her-name

OVER the years I've spent some time addressing groups on the two or three subjects about which I seem to know something. The object has been to teach and/or entertain the audience but in actuality it often turns out that I'm the one who ends up learning something. For instance, I've come to the realization that you can't be thin skinned and go out on the speaking circuit. Here is just a sampling of examples leading me to this conclusion.

A few years ago (and it remains indelible on my memory) I was asked to speak about the poet Emily Dickinson at a retirement home. Unbeknownst to me at the time, there was a gentleman living there who acted as their chief critic—the home's version of Hollywood's film reviewer, Roger Ebert. The program that day consisted of both speaking and singing, so after I'd done both for a while our critic, who had nodded off, suddenly came to and blurted out, "Gawd! Is that woman still talking? I thought she was going to sing something!" On subsequent awakenings he would bellow, "Is she still here? When are we getting the refreshments!" Somehow it wasn't his utterings that hurt so much—it was his dragging out his watch and shaking it to see whether it was still working.

You would think historical societies would be safe places to speak. They are generally located in interesting old buildings that lend themselves to what I do. There are exceptions, however, as I learned one night when I arrived in a central Massachusetts town to find that their historical society was in a modern ranch house. Actually it was in *half* of a ranch house. The other half was occupied by the local police department. Unfortunately, it was a beastly hot summer night and because they'd just painted all the windows shut we had to keep the front door open in order to let in ten million mosquitos and a few breaths of air. To top it off, crime was at an all time high in the little town that night and cruisers came and went, sirens blared and wrong do-ers of all descriptions kept being hauled up the front steps for interrogation. If you like challenges, try talking about a poet with all that going on. Believe me, pick-pockets, perverts and poetry don't mix.

How about a nice family campground? One summer I was invited to speak at one of those, and my instructions from the program chairman said to park "next to the latrine." My friend who went with me chided me on the way down as to how such a "star" could be expected to park by a latrine. By the time we got there I'd begun to think she might have something there, so I pulled the car into a spot near the all-purpose building where I would be speaking. We could see folks carrying in casseroles and desserts for the potluck supper which would precede the program.

I was unpacking the car when a gentleman came along and told me, politely, that I couldn't park there. "You should park down by the latrine!" So much for star quality.

But this wasn't the end of it. I always tell program chairmen that I prefer not to eat before speaking. Unfortunately, this time I neglected to take into consideration the fact that these people were fantastic cooks and the friend who accompanied me hadn't had any supper.

"Don't worry," I said, "someone will ask us whether we'd like something to eat."

We waited. We watched. THEY ate.

Finally we got up and went into the kitchen to help ourselves to coffee. While there we spied the most tantalizing array of home made pies we'd ever laid eyes on. "Surely," I said, "they will invite us to have dessert, right?" Wrong. It was a long night. To make matters worse, our trip back from Massachusetts was a late one with not one open eatery in sight. I decided that for the future I might have to rethink my no-food policy—especially if they are going to serve pie.

One of my most challenging experiences came the time I was asked to speak at a men's lodge convention.

"Are you sure they'd want to listen to me talking about a poet—wouldn't they rather see some young thing jump out of a cake?" I asked the chairman. He checked with the committee and for some reason, they still wanted me (perhaps they thought I *was* going to jump out of a cake.) So on a Friday night, I made my way to a hotel in another city where I was scheduled for 8:30pm.

When I pulled up to the hotel's function wing it was dark and quiet, and the corridor smelled of decades worth of Marlboros and Camels. After I lugged my guitar, music stand and books inside, I was told that the men were having their lodge meeting so I waited outside the room. Suddenly an elevator door opened and out spilled an assortment of women, high spirited and laughing; some with drinks in their hands and others with lodge hats on. These, I surmised, were the wives.

At first I was relieved to think there would be women attending—they would be much more receptive to hearing songs and stories about a woman poet. But then it came.

"Do we *have* to go to this thing?" one of them complained. "Who wants to sit around on a Friday night listening to someone talk when we could be up in the hospitality room enjoying ourselves!"

There was agreement all around. I could have crawled through a crack in the floor and taken my paraphernalia with me.

All at once the doors to the room opened and out poured the lodge members, wearing red fezes and looking tired and harried after their meeting. Most were in a hurry as they brushed past me heading for either the Men's Room or the Hospitality Room or both. Trusting that they would come back (and they did), I finally began my program at 9:25pm. I hadn't gotten too far into the presentation when an elderly gentleman entered the room, took an empty chair directly in front of me and proceeded to fall sound asleep. Now I could put up with a little snoring. What I couldn't take, however, was the woman across the room who kept jumping up from her seat and running down the aisle to wake the gent up every so often. Now that hurt.

In all fairness, those lodge members and wives were very polite, considering it was a Friday night and the hospitality room was beckoning. To this day, though, I still say those men would have much preferred the girl jumping out of a cake.

I could go on. Like the night I slipped and tore an Achilles tendon just before driving to a school performance 40 miles away and finally getting to the emergency room at midnight; or the evening I was invited to speak on Dickinson in a woman's bedroom, only to discover when I got there that she'd invited men only; and then there was the stormy night I spoke at a large city library and only three people showed up—two of whom were relatives!

Despite these and other ego wrecking experiences out on the speakers' circuit, I still say there is nothing like the challenge of getting up at a podium and interacting with an audience, even on days when the program chairman rises to introduce you and forgets who you are—and take it from me, it's happened!

A New England town meeting dilemma

I'M AFRAID I've attended my last Town Meeting. I hate to say this because I enjoy town meetings. I like to study them with a Margaret Mead eye; observing the emerging personalities, watching for last minute lobbying, and counting the number of people who for the life of them can't find their ballot cards when it's time for the vote. I'll miss all these things.

My decision to bid good-bye to Town Meetings has nothing to do with politics, by the way. It has to do with the chairs.

You see, a couple of years ago our town hall got refurbished. The walls and ceiling got painted, the floors refinished and even the outside was spiffed up—and if they'd stopped there, I wouldn't be in this predicament today, but they didn't. They went on to purchase new chairs.

Now these new chairs are actually rather nice—they even have padded seats. My problem has to do with how the chairs are set up. They aren't just placed *near* each other in rows as the old wooden ones were. These chairs are designed so they are somehow locked together with not a scintilla of space existing between your chair and the one next to you. You couldn't slip a piece of tissue paper between your body and your neighbor's if you tried. This means that if you didn't know the people seated next to you at the beginning of the meeting, you can be sure you'll be on intimate terms with them by the time the Moderator bangs the final gavel. This cozy seating arrangement brings a whole new meaning to the term "cheek by jowl."

The folks who purchased these chairs are no doubt slim of hip, otherwise, how could they possibly not have foreseen the crushing situation they were creating? In all fairness to this

Chair Committee, however, nowhere in the town statistics is there reference to townspeople's girth.

So now here we are with rows of chairs that defy many of us to sit on them for four or five hours without letting any of our adipose tissue extend over into the other person's space. Let me tell you, it isn't easy. We may be able to draw in our stomachs by some deep inhaling but I assure you it doesn't work when it comes to broad hips because believe me, I've tried it. Somehow brain waves to that part of the body seem to have become short-circuited. My cellulite just doesn't get the message that I want it to shrink back, move over, contract.

Let me add here, that I am far from the broadest person in town. I have observed that other folks, wider of shoulder or beam, have the same if not worse problem than I have. When someone settles into the seat next to them, they have to pull in their extremities—uncross their legs, tuck their elbows in close to the body, fold their newspaper in quarters, and clutch their town report tightly to their chest—just so they won't annoy their neighbor.

At my last town meeting, I finally confirmed something I had already suspected. I got out a ruler and measured the empty seat in front of me.

"Aha," I said to my embarrassed friends, "just as I thought! The seat measures a scant 15 inches across . . . and I'll bet you that more than half the people in this town measure more than that when in a seated position!"

That night, out of curiosity, I got out a yardstick, sat down on it and did a little measuring of my own. Suffice it to say, the people who bought these narrow chairs never had me in mind when they did the ordering.

I've been told that the reason for these clamp-together chairs has to do with *firelaws*. Maybe they figure that in case of fire it will take us so long to disentangle ourselves from the people next to us that we'll at least avoid a sudden stampede toward the exits.

Anyway, the thought of not participating in further Town Meetings isn't a happy one and I suppose there is one possible solution. Those of us who measure more than 15" across, extending beyond the edges of the new chairs, could do some serious exercising and dieting before the next meeting rolls around.

I figure it's either *that,* or the town will just have to give us tax abatements to help defray the cost of liposuction. Suddenly the words LIVE FREE OR DIE have taken on a whole new meaning.

It's no deal for me

I'VE BEEN playing cards with Pauline, Michelle and Ben a lot lately, but to tell you the truth, they are beginning to wear on me. In fact, I'm just plain sick of the three of them. I sense that Pauline is going through the menopause, Michelle is always out to beat me at any cost, and Ben, well, although I suppose he's cute, he doesn't seem to have any personality.

These aren't real people; they are programmed into my computer. When I bought the thing I must have bought them too. This means that every time I type in that I want to play a certain card game, these three show up uninvited. I don't pretend to know how this occurs. I just hope that when I shut down the computer, they don't suffocate in there.

If any of my friends got wind of this they'd be picking themselves up off the floor by now because they know perfectly well that I don't play cards.

I don't make apologies for this shortcoming, by the way. I happen to feel that we are not responsible for the brains we are dealt; they came with the rest of our bodies as packaged deals. We never got a chance to place an order for a certain model. Consequently the brain I drew doesn't seem to have the capacity to remember—or CARE —who played which card, who bid what or whose turn it is to deal. When any of the above happen, my mind wanders to other things like the room decor, how many peanuts are left in the snack dish, or the fact that I want to get the game over with and go home.

One night I was invited to a friend's home for dinner and was asked to bring along a little change for a game after the meal. When anyone says the word "game" to me I want to get on a one-way flight out of the country. My blood pressure shoots up in anticipation of being locked into something that I enjoy less than George Bush likes broccoli. Sure enough, that

19

night after dinner the hostess whisked off the table cover and replaced it with one that had lines painted on it, similar to a gambling wheel. Well, I about died. I kept asking if I couldn't go out to the kitchen and do the dishes or something, but she'd hear nothing of it.

My initial fear was well founded. It turned out to be not one game but two, where you switch from one to the other . It was a nightmare for me. All my change disappeared faster than you could say "Gorin," while the woman next to me could have used a Brinks truck to take home her winnings.

I came from a card playing family so somewhere something went drastically wrong. For my father and mother, getting together with the Hogans one night a week for a game of cards was right up there with the Saturday night bath and watching the Hit Parade. My sisters and brother are good at cards too. But somehow the Bridge, Cribbage and Poker genes came to a screeching halt just before I was born. Consequently, I play simple games on the computer, where no one will know how bad I really am.

One of the easy games I play is Hearts. It looked simple enough when I pulled it up on the computer screen—at least I thought it was, until the other day.

I was talking to a friend on the phone when she happened to mention that she'd just been playing a card game on her computer.

"Well, that's a coincidence," I said, "so was I." (I didn't ask her whether she knew Pauline, Michelle and Ben.)

"But I thought you HATED cards."

"Well, it's not that I hate them, I'm just not mentally geared to play the game, at least not with real people. BUT I've found this simple game of Hearts and it's great. What's so fantastic about it is that I am always winning!"

"You are? When I play on my computer I sure don't always win," said my friend.

"Well, these three dodos I'm playing with keep giving me high cards, and lots of hearts, besides. Isn't that great? It takes me NO time to get the score up to 100."

There is a loud screeching noise on the other end of the phone. It is laughter—uncontrollable laughter.

"You're not winning—you're LOSING!" my friend screamed. "In Hearts, the object is to be left with the lowest score not the highest . . . and with as few hearts as possible!"

Suddenly Pauline, Michelle and Ben didn't look so dumb. I'd been underestimating them for weeks. They probably sensed all along that they were playing with a rookie with a writer's brain. As for me, I suddenly knew how Kasparov felt going up against Deep Blue.

The poet Emily Dickinson used to say—"I wonder what the OTHER people do"? Well, one of the things the OTHER people do is play cards. I envy them in a way but I am not so foolhardy as to dare to try to join them, however..

No. I'm sticking with Pauline, Michelle and Ben—if after all I've said about them, they'll still have me!

Woes of a yard sale

IT'S SATURDAY morning and you're driving along minding your own business when suddenly the car ahead of you jams on the brakes and you nearly plow into it. Once you've regained your composure, you ask yourself what kind of a driver would stop dead in the street for no apparent reason?

I'll tell you what kind of driver—a YARD SALE driver! They pull over to the side without the slightest warning because somewhere in someone's roadside mass of furniture, bric-a-brac and just plain junk, they've spotted a lamp that would be just perfect in their living room.

There ought to be signs posted near all yard sales—CAU-TION—YARD SALE SHOPPERS PULLING OVER.

Yard sale shoppers have one thing in common; they are certain they will find some priceless item in your yard sale that you were dumb enough to put a 40 cent sticker on. To them, yard saling is the modern version of panning for gold; the fact that they enjoy themselves in the process seems to outweigh the fact that they hardly ever hit the mother lode.

Actually *having* a yard sale is a lot scarier than shopping at one. First of all, it's work. All those sale items don't just magically appear in your front yard. Putting on one of these sales is not for the faint of heart or weak of back.

Of course, if you have a yard sale you are bound to have Early Birds. Now, here is an interesting group for you. These are the folks who start cruising your neighborhood at dawn, with their newspaper listings in hand—the ones that say "No Early Birds Allowed."

By about 8AM when you are lugging the stuff out of your garage, you notice that the early birds are back. They are parked across the street, eating their donuts, drinking their coffee and pretending not to notice the items you are setting up.

Along about 8:30 they get brave and amble up onto your driveway and start pawing over the goods. "Oh, you don't begin until 9 o'clock? We could swear the paper said 8." Oh sure, folks! By the time the sale actually starts you feel as if you know these people, they've been hanging around so long. Worse yet, by now they've sized up your merchandise and know what's good, what's fake and which of your grandmother's teacups have cracks in them.

I know all this because I am a veteran of a couple of yard sales myself. After my last one I vowed never to have one again, and after I tell you what happened, you'll see why.

The sale started out pretty well. It was a sunny day, most of the shoppers were good-natured, and someone with a pickup truck even showed up to take away my old two-ton sleep sofa and matching recliner.

Then it happened. Around 3 o'clock in the afternoon, as things were winding down, this late model Oldsmobile drove up and three well-dressed women got out. I sized them up as salt and pepper shaker collector types—or maybe just "lookers."

Shortly after they began looking over the merchandise, we noticed that one of them left the others to walk across the lawn to the further side of the house. Curious to see where she would be going, we followed her. When she got to the corner of the house and behind a large bush, she proceeded to relieve herself of her morning coffee! Right there on my lawn, this nicely dressed, pleasant looking lady was watering my rhododendrons!

Her excuse: she'd been visiting yard sales since early morning, with no time to stop. My reply: she could have asked me to use the facilities; I might have said yes —for a fee.

No sir and no ma'am, I don't plan to have another yard sale anytime soon. For those of you who do, however, I offer this advice: get organized, price realistically, and be on the lookout for three well dressed women driving a late model Oldsmobile!

No more stopping by woods

MY SISTER and I were sitting in McDonald's having a McGrilled Chicken and coffee when she suddenly exclaimed, "Look! Did you see that? Those people pulled into the parking lot, went straight to the rest rooms and then went right back out to their cars without buying a single thing! Can you believe it?"

I glanced out the window just in time to observe one well-coiffed, white-haired female and two equally distinguished looking gents climbing back into their Oldsmobile sedan. From the looks of them they were probably headed for an afternoon bridge game.

"Yes," I replied, "I can believe it!"

"Well, I think it's nervy. Not even buying a measly cup of coffee!"

I began to question the logic of that statement, saying that perhaps they bought the last cup of coffee at *another* McDonald's down the road and that's why they had to stop at *this* one. "Besides, if you drank a cup of coffee at every McDonald's you stopped at, you'd have yourself a mighty vicious cycle," I said.

"Look, there goes another one!" (I could see I was getting nowhere.)

As we worked our way through lunch, the rest room parade watch continued and I could sense my sister's blood pressure rising. My fear was that she might decide to station herself outside the rest room doors, asking for proof that these travelers did indeed plan to purchase something at the counter before leaving—a muffin, a Happy Meal, *something!* I had visions of people running back to their cars in unrelieved distress, all because of my sister.

Somehow, the fact that people do occasionally stop and

use rest rooms at fast food places comes as no surprise to me—especially the traveling public. McDonald's has become the alternative to (if Robert Frost will forgive me) stopping by (the) woods on a snowy evening.

Let's face it. Straining bladders have been the cause of drivers pulling over to the sides of roads for years. Before I knew better, I used to wonder why it was that so many more men than women were interested in getting out of their cars to look at the scenery. Of course, I eventually found out that it had less to do with nature appreciation than with nature's configuration.

One day, my four-year-old grandson told me rather proudly that on a recent out-of-state trip, when he could wait no longer, his dad just pulled the car over and told him that in emergencies it's okay to go "right there on the grass!!" To him, this was like a rite of passage (no pun intended)—definitely a guy thing.

Now that the McDonald's of the world have come to the rescue, who knows how much grass and how many trees they've saved thanks to those rest rooms. Perhaps they should get an environmentalist award.

Just imagine how many man and woman hours it must take (at minimum wage) to keep all those public rest rooms neat and tidy all day long. Cleaning up after "the public" is no fun. I know this for a fact because I graduated from the Duncanson Grove School of Outhouse Cleaners.

You see, my husband's family once owned a picnic grove, which they often rented out for large summer outings—the kind where the beer flowed, the barbecues never quit, and the steady stream of humanity marching to and from the rest rooms was endless. I used the term rest rooms loosely, for those facilities were outhouses with a capital "O" and it was our job to clean them after each outing. This was no easy feat since the nearest running water was more than 50 yards away.

The newspaper code of decency prohibits me from going into detail here. Let's just say that the next time you feel put-upon cleaning your own bathrooms with those fancy sweet-smelling sprays and sponges, think of me in those "ladies' rooms," scrubbing splintery wood, sweeping floors, and last but not least, shoveling in good old lime. My husband used to say it built character. If that's the case, during those summers I must have built up enough character to last a lifetime.

Those duties made me acutely aware of how careless and thoughtless we all become when we step into the role of *the public*. That's why I have such deep respect for the McDonald's employees who tidy up after the rest of us. In fact, even though they have a no-tipping policy, I think there should be an exception for this latrine duty, don't you?

Corporate-wise, I'm certain their rest room popularity comes as no surprise to the likes of Mr. Mac and Mr. Donald or Mr. Burger and Mr. King. They probably sat in some board rooms long ago projecting what percentage of the motoring public would use their rest rooms without ever visiting the take-out counter. Then they weighed the cost of this against the goodwill they would engender, and voted to fold the cost into their public relations budget.

McDonald's and their counterparts are often given a bad rap by towns that view them as eyesores or undesirables. They somehow disregard the fact that besides offering food at reasonable prices and some much-needed jobs, they have other saving graces—not the least of which are those harbingers of hope on the highways, the rest rooms.

So, on behalf of the weak bladders along our highways and byways, I would like to extend a long overdue thank-you to these often maligned fast food highway pit stops. And to think that all these years we were under the impression that *Rolaids* spelled relief. Now it turns out that relief is really spelled M-C-D-O-N-A-L-D-S.

I'm a poet and didn't know it

WE ALL succumb to temptation once in a while and my time came a while back when I weakened and answered a little newspaper advertisement for a poetry contest. It said that all I had to do was send in one of my poems and sit back to wait for fame and fortune to roll in.

I didn't really expect to win anything, but lo and behold, in about a month I got a letter—or poetry-gram—from a woman named Emma Lou Sonnet (names changed to protect the innocent or guilty).

It seems that Emma Lou headed up the poetry contest section of the Acme Poetry Society and she informed me that my little poem had somehow managed to garner an honorable mention in the contest! She went on to tell me that she *loved* the poem and she *loved* me because I was a poet. There was something suspicious about this letter, but who was I to mistrust a woman named Emmal Lou who *loved* poets?

Shortly, I received an official citation bearing Emma Lou's name at the bottom, proclaiming to all the world that Joann Snow Duncanson's poem won honorable mention. I figured it was the last I would hear about this whole thing, but not so.

The letter was followed up by another poetry-gram from Emma Lou, telling me that since my poem was a Golden Award winner, I was now eligible to have it published in a World Treasury of Golden Poems. Apparently my little poem went from Honorable Mention to Golden Award caliber almost overnight! Surely this verse and I were on our way somewhere big.

Then I read further and found that although Emma Lou still loved me, in order to be in the book I would have to *buy* the book to the tune of $39.50! And if I wanted my photo to accompany the poem, it would cost another $45.

After a month of soul searching, I decided to make Emma Lou happy and myself famous by sending my hard earned money to the Acme Poetry Society; I would forego, however, the photo and have a bare-bones version of my little poem standing bravely on the page all by itself.

Not long after this, guess what arrived in my mailbox? No, not the book, but another poetry-gram from Emma Lou telling me that as a Silver Poet Award winner (now I'd gone from Honorable Mention to Golden to Silver), I was invited to attend their annual Poetry convention in Las Vegas.

According to Emma Lou, their Board of Directors chose *my* poem from those submitted over the past four years— rather awesome considering the Society has 1.4 million members! Not only would I receive a commemorative trophy, but I should report to the Las Vegas Hilton where I would be given two minutes to read my poem and make a statement. Emma Lou advised me to dress formally because Bob Hope was to be the keynote speaker.

Then, if this weren't enough, they were planning a Parade of Poets. I began picturing what a parade of poets would look like; would they dress up as Edgar Alan Poe's and Edna St. Vincent Millay's? THEN—and this is the *piece d'resistance*— there would be a poetry balloon-a-thon where my little poem (and 3000 others) would drift aloft to faraway places, spreading iambic pentameter wherever it chanced to land!

I pondered the invitation carefully. Was this thing for real? Poetry in Las Vegas? How much would this little ego boosting trip cost me?

Finally the decision was made; Bob Hope would have to wing it without me. But I could at least bask in the knowledge that my little poem, "Widows Don't Dance at the Weddings," was an *Honorable Mention, Golden* AND *Silver* award winning poem. I mention the poem's name just in case at some future date Steven Spielberg decides to make a movie of it, or PBS runs it as a mini-series, or I become Poet Laureate of the United States.

After all—anything can happen if Emma Lou *loves* you!

There's one born every minute

SOMETHING interesting arrived in the mail the other day. It came as a result of my entering Emma Lou Sonnet's poetry contest.

Against my better judgment, I let my yearning for fame overtake me and I opted to purchase the book in which my poem was to be printed. Understand, that if I hadn't agreed to buy the book, my poem wouldn't BE in the book.

Even though I was skeptical, I admit to being excited as I unwrapped the leather bound volume that would feature my poem. I leafed through the pages. Guess how many of us "award winning" poets shelled out money to have our poems in this book. Seven THOUSAND, that's how many! This means that 7,000 poems were crammed onto the pages, with printing so small even the Hubble telescope would have trouble reading them.

Let's face it, I and 6,999 other poets had been had!

This was almost as embarrassing as the time I looked into that condo time-sharing offer on Cape Cod. Usually I deep-six these get-rich-quick schemes mailed to my house, but somehow on that occasion my curiosity got the best of me. It sounded like a good deal.

"We are pleased to notify you of your selection as a Merchandise Recipient in our Eastern Region promotion for "The Sea Shell" on Cape Cod. Even if your award number does not match #1 (Pontiac Grand Prix), #2 ($2,000), or #3 (Regal Microwave—Bake and Roast Grill), you will still be a big winner . . . your family will receive their choice of a VHS video cassette recorder or $250 cash . . . blah blah . . ."

After reading the letter several times I decided that if these people were dumb enough to give something away, I might as well be the person they give it to.

So I called Helen.

Helen is a friend who has put up with my idiosyncrasies for many years, so why not one more?

"Come on, Helen, just come to the Sea Shell for a short presentation and I'll take you out for dinner on the winnings afterward. You don't have to worry that I'll be tempted to buy a time-share either."

Now Helen is a very wise person. She knew that it had to be a scam, but she agreed to go along.

On Friday we drove to the Sea Shell only to find it situated right smack alongside the most congested portion of the Cape, in a run down, defunct chain motel.

I said to Helen, "Are you sure we've got the right place?" She had a knowing look on her face as she assured me that this was indeed where I was planning to pick up my VCR or $250.

I looked around at the makeshift fence surrounding the property and the remnants of an outdoor swimming pool where only a few vestiges of chipped blue paint clung to its sides. I began to have my doubts.

Just then a personable gentlemen came over and introduced himself, calling me by name as if he were either a long lost relative or at least an old classmate. He took us inside where several other folks were gathered, and I began to hope they had enough prizes to go around.

Our salesman talked and talked about how lovely it would be to own a time-share at the Sea Shell. Helen, figuring she would help shorten the agony, began asking how much a unit would cost. Somewhat annoyed, the salesman made it very clear that this information could not be divulged just yet.

Much to our dismay, we sat and listened to him for almost two hours. Next came the tour. After making our way past the chaos in the hallways due to renovations, I found the units themselves had some saving graces. High ceilings with paddle fans, modern kitchens, large mirrored panels which disguised Murphy beds, pulling down out of the walls.

Helen, seeing signs of my weakening, resumed asking, "How much?"

Finally the tour ended and we got our answer. The least expensive 2 1/2 room unit was $10,000. Although it probably came as no surprise to our salesman, I broke the news that I was not interested.

Then, as if I needed any reminding, he told me that I was entitled to a prize, and led us to the gift room. (Mentally I was deciding whether Helen's car trunk would hold a microwave or not).

I looked around the tiny room and said, "I wonder where they store all the microwaves and VCRs." After matching my lucky number to the prize list on the computer, the clerk announced, "Congratulations! You have won #3!"

"Number 3, " I exclaimed, "that's the microwave!" In no time the clerk returned, carrying a thin brown box measuring about nine 9 inches wide, 11 inches long and 1 inch deep.

"Here's your prize!" said he. On the box it said *Imperial Regal Microwave* (and then in small letters) *Cookware—Roast and Grill*. Inside the box was a tiny microwave cooking tray on which to cook bacon! Probably had a retail value of about $1.99.

I didn't dare look at Helen as I carried my microwave cookware out to the car because I knew she would have the words "I told you so" written all over her face.

Well, that was a few years ago. I'm sure Helen thinks I've grown up since then and learned from my mistake. But listen, we are all entitled to lapses now and then, aren't we? Falling for Emma Lou's poetry book idea was definitely one of mine!

There is one born every minute.

From the mouths of babes

SOMETIMES I'm in the right place at the right time and sometimes in the wrong place at the wrong time. I'll leave it up to you to decide which applies in this case, after you've read what comes next.

I was just sitting at a lunch counter a few towns away from here, minding my own business, when a good looking young man came bounding into the restaurant, leaned over the counter and gave an equally good looking waitress a big hug and kiss. Obviously glad to see each other, they caught up on what was new.

"You look great!"

"How long are you home for?"

"How's Boston?"

So far the conversation was nothing to write home about. But then the course of the dialogue took a decided turn.

"Oh, wow!" the good looking waitress exclaimed. "When did you have it done? Does it hurt? Oh, wow!"

By now, some of his friends around the other side of the counter became curious and called the young man over so they could see him at close range. He obliged, and soon more exclamations could be heard throughout the restaurant. More "Oh, wow's!" but an equal number of "How disgusting's!" joined the chorus.

By now I begin to sense a story here so I ask the good looking waitress if she thinks her friend would mind coming over to talk with me. I explained that I'm a columnist and I thought it would be interesting to find out just what everyone was exclaiming over—maybe I could write him up.

Probably figuring I was on assignment from the National Enquirer, she rushed over to deliver my message, pointing at me while she talked. The good looking object of everyone's attention hesitated a minute, peering at me across the restaurant, no doubt trying to figure how anyone who looks like me works for the Enquirer.

Eventually he came over, as I knew he would. After all, anyone daring enough to merit so many "Oh, wow's!" would certainly dare to talk with little old me.

When he got closer, I could see that he was not without adornment. In one ear there was an impressive array of gold earrings—hoops on the earlobe and studs higher up. But that couldn't be what all the fuss was about. These days a lot of people have more holes in their ears than God intended, so I studied him further for something more unique.

Yes, there was one more embellishment, a gold ring in his left nostril. I was definitely on to something, but I was quite sure this wasn't it either.

"I couldn't help notice all the attention you've been getting since you came into this place," I began. "You obviously have something that nobody else around here has but I'm not sure what it is. It's not your earrings is it?"

"Nope."

"Is it your nose ring?"

"Nope."

By now I start to squirm in my seat wondering whether I was going to get into territory better left undisturbed. Then it came.

"I had my tongue pierced."

Now the good news was that I had finished my lunch when he made this announcement. The bad news was that I wasn't at all sure it had time to digest.

"Your tongue, you say?" I stammered. "You got your tongue pierced?"

Then I launched into some small talk about how I've always admired people who were brave enough to deviate from the norm and express their individuality by having themselves tattooed or shaving their heads or . . .

I was obviously stalling for time until I got the nerve to ask the next question, but it had to come eventually.

"May I see it?"

So right there at the lunch counter, in view of who knows who, he stuck his (by now famous) tongue out at me.

"Oh wow!" I heard my mouth saying while my brain was definitely siding with those other people who were saying, "How disgusting!"

It was not a pretty sight.

About one inch straight back from the tip of his tongue there was indeed a hole that went clear down through to the under side. It was about a quarter of an inch in diameter and looked as if someone had taken a single-hole paper punch to it. In the hole was a shiny device that resembled a barbell—maybe an inch long. I suppose if the thing were stationary and secured I wouldn't have minded so much but this was loose and it bobbed up and down when he talked. I could only imagine the gyrations it went through when he was eating a hamburger and fries.

I thought to myself, you got him over here smarty, so now what can you ask this free spirit?

"Where did you have your—well that is, where did you have IT done?" Live Free Or Die notwithstanding, I somehow couldn't picture a tongue piercer setting up shop in this little New Hampshire town.

"I had it done in Boston. Body piercing is pretty big in cities. Ears, noses, eyebrows, lips, necks . . ."

I stopped him there because somehow I didn't care if I ever found out what other parts of one's anatomy could be pierced.

I suddenly became acutely aware of my own tongue and how throughout this whole conversation it seemed to take on greater and greater significance. I felt it inching back toward my throat, probably in fear that I was getting ideas here.

"Would you mind my asking how much it cost? Not that I'm thinking of having it done, you understand, but some of my readers might."

He told me that the piercing itself cost only $20, and that the barbell piece made out of stainless steel cost $50.

By this time I figured I'd kept this star away from his public long enough. Time is precious when you're a young guy home for just a weekend. But I had one more question which I was saving for last.

"Has Mom seen it?"

He shot me a knowing glance and smiled. I think he knew I was wondering how I'd deal with it if my own son came home with a holey tongue.

"I showed it to her this weekend, and she wasn't crazy about it but she wasn't all that surprised either. After all, she's used to me by now—I started with the pierced ears four years ago."

I thanked him for talking with me and he went back over to sit with his friends in the booth, probably telling them that he was going to be in the National Enquirer. He was talking animatedly and I could picture that tongue apparatus bobbing up and down with his every word.

The waitress had brought me some fresh coffee but somehow or other, I couldn't muster the appetite for it so I paid my bill and left.

Now this is where I should wind up my story by saying something profound about how to deal with differing lifestyles or what to do if your offspring or grandchild comes home with earrings in his or her nose or eyebrow or, perish the thought—tongue—but I can't.

You're going to have to draw your own conclusions here because believe it or not, for once in my life I'm speechless. In fact, you might even say I'm tongue-tied.

Where IS that kitchen anyway?

SOMETIMES I like to think about cooking. I don't actually *do* much cooking, you understand, but I like to *think* about it.

If memory serves me right, cooking was when we went to the store and bought things known as ingredients—raw, unprepared items which, when put together with others and heated at the right temperature, resulted in a meal served at something we once called dinner time. You remember dinner time; when we actually had a meal that came out of the oven rather than a carton, and it was served at an hour when everyone in the family was home.

I seem to recall that we sat down together—at the same time, in the same room—for an uninterrupted period of time. This was before phone companies and banking institutions got the bright idea to call us as soon as we unfolded our napkin and began passing the Hamburger Helper.

Today, dinner time with completely home cooked food is for many of us just a fading memory. I am the first to admit that my own kitchen has long since become a mausoleum; a nice place to visit but I certainly don't want to live there. When I decide to entertain—which seems to happen less and less frequently—I almost need a road map to show me where the kitchen is. A plot plan to tell me where the utensils are stored wouldn't be a bad idea, either.

One day a while ago, I fell into a domestic mood and put together a beef stew and whipped up a batch of lemonade cookies. Willy Wordsworth didn't know what to make of it. He considers the kitchen his room because he's the only one who eats there with any regularity—after all, cat food gets served without fail, and you don't have to cook it! But here I was, actually rummaging around for pans, making noise with the blender, and doing all sorts of unnatural things. Soon interesting but foreign odors began emanating from my oven. Willy stared and inhaled in disbelief the rest of the day.

Once you are out of the habit of cooking, but in a wild moment invite folks over for a meal, a sense of panic can overtake you. It's not doing the actual cooking itself that is difficult, for that can actually be enjoyable. It's deciding what to have for a menu that's the problem.

My recipe decisions are based on a very simple formula; I get out my ruler and measure the list of ingredients. If it measures more than two inches—i.e., many ingredients and multiple preparatory steps—you can be sure my guests aren't going to sink their teeth into that particular goody at my house! This is nothing to be proud of, by the way, but it is a fact of life.

I once wrote about one of my cookbooks, *White Trash Cooking*, quoting several of the down home recipes it features. I received a scathing letter from a local woman asking how dare I make fun of those poor white women. Well lady, the sad truth was I wasn't making fun of them. I *like* some of those recipes and envy their simplicity. For instance Grand Canyon Cake: "2 boxes of plain white cake mix, 2 cans of chocolate icing and 1 cup of whisky sauce. Bake the cake, frost it, then poke holes in it and pour in the whiskey sauce." These folks are on my culinary wavelength—brevity is their password! Except for the fact that they use a lot of lard and collard greens, they are my kind of people.

There are three basic reasons why Americans don't do as much cooking any more. First, they simply don't have time. Kids, jobs, and other activities have forced us into culinary shortcuts. Second, supermarkets have made it too easy for us. For instance, I recently saw packages of prepared mashed potato down at the local A&P. Not boxes of dried potato flakes, and not frozen potato—I mean cartons of the real mashed kind—ready to heat and eat. I couldn't believe my eyes.

Then, even more decadent, over in the next aisle was *prepared Jell-O*. I guess the manufacturers have decided that boiling water and adding a few crystals is beyond us somehow. I may be a lazy cook, but I draw the line at premashed potato and prejelled Jell-O.

And now for the third reason we don't cook from scratch any more. In my house, it is brown, sits on my kitchen counter, and bakes a potato in five minutes. The microwave oven has replaced cooking with what can only be called "heating up." We heat up frozen foods, we heat up chicken from the deli counter, we heat up Stauffer's lasagna, et cetera. Fast foods and the microwave make for a liberating, time-saving combination, but at the same time they tempt us away from the real thing.

Real cooking is therapeutic. There is something about the feel of the ingredients in our hands, the rhythm of the steps in the preparation, the aromas that fill our kitchens, and beholding the final product, that is an exercise difficult to duplicate. For some of us, however, these experiences become less and less frequent. I confess that I find cooking for one person—myself—boring and not too high on my list of priorities. Though I find my occasional culinary dabbling like a visit with an old friend, I'd much rather spend my time writing than marinating mushrooms or making meat loaf.

Here is a word of advice to those who find themselves in the same cooking slump that I am in. Surround yourselves with people who still know where their kitchens are, and what to do in them. With any luck, they will invite you over once in a while just so you won't forget what a complete meal looks like. In return, try to be charming, witty and openly grateful. It sometimes works for me—give it a try.

Lately I've been trying to think of a place to go on vacation this year. It just occurred to me that I could always spend it in my kitchen, After all, it would be a change of scene.

No such thing as a good square meal

AS A child I was one of the fussiest eaters on earth. I was made to sit there long after the others had left the table, and told to finish the by then cold and clammy meat and vegetables *or else*. It wasn't until I got away from home and no one told me I *had* to eat my vegetables, that I began to like food . . . well, *most* foods.

I *do* have this hangup about square food. You see, I just don't happen to think that *any* food was ever meant to be served square. Engineered and manufactured objects are square, but things that are grown to eat? Not as far as I'm concerned. There's something about introducing an object with distinct corners to a digestive system which doesn't have a single right angle to it that seems contrary to nature somehow.

Take carrots, for instance. There is no earthly reason for these colorful tubers to ever appear on our plates in the shape of little squares. Yet, some gremlin somewhere is always turning them into tiny cubes and sneaking them in amongst servings of perfectly respectable green peas (a veggie which, thankfully, no one's been able to square off yet). The peas were doing all right by themselves until those orange cubes came along.

I grew up near a farm, but so help me I never saw a square turkey or pig, yet turkey and ham are very apt to turn up in the deli department in squares. There ought to be a law!

Even some hamburgers are square these days. A bad idea—especially when served on round buns so that the fat drips off the four corners onto your shirt.

Some breads, of course, are square. An unnatural state of affairs if I ever saw one. Bread is supposed to be free flowing—rising up and rounding into wonderfully unpre-

39

dictable contours—no two loaves the same. But no. In their wisdom, some enterprising bakers came along and concocted what they call the sandwich loaf. I suppose this is to fit those perfectly square turkey and ham slices mentioned above.

Even the dessert department is guilty. A friend of mine enjoys making angel food cakes, and they come out perfect except for one thing—they are square. This is because she happens to own one of the few square angel food cake pans in captivity. I keep telling her she should donate the thing to the Smithsonian, but so far she's not taking me up on it. Angel food cakes come under the category of comfort food and in my view, that means rounded, soft and eater-friendly, not square.

I can't even get away from the square bread phenomenon in church. When it's communion time and the elements are being passed among the flock, guess what's on the trays? Square pieces of bread. Some Sundays it is so perfectly cut that I swear those deacons must have a slide rule out in the church kitchen. To me, there's something uninviting and clinical about perfectly chiseled squares of bread—even in church. I like it better when they offer us a broken loaf where we can pull off asymmetrical pieces of the real thing.

Here's another one—fish. Fish should never be square either. No self respecting salmon or halibut would want to be caught dead being served as a perfectly square fishwich or fish-a-ma-jig—or even oblong fish sticks, for that matter. How insulting to a creature with such graceful contours.

Pizza—now there's something that we always think of as round, yet someone—probably the same person who dreamed up my friend's angel food cake pan—decided to make it into a perfect square. I don't know about you, but to me pizza doesn't taste the same if it doesn't have round edges.

Since I'm not much of a meat eater, I occasionally look for substitutes on a menu. Tofu for instance. But in order for me to enjoy it, tofu has to be camouflaged beyond recognition. It should be blended in with the rest of the dish, absorbing the flavor of its pot-mates. Occasionally, I'll order tofu only to have it arrive on my plate as one firm, slimy square.

One look and it is enough to make me revert to my pot roast and gravy ways.

I've never seen anyone dig up a square potato but sure enough, they often show up at the table that way—diced for potato salad or as cubes floating in clam chowder like so many little packing crates drifting in the sea.

Take my word for it, square food has been making definite inroads in our society: Jell-O cubes, geometric fruit cocktail, croutons, waffles, frosted mini-wheats—even my cat's food is beginning to come in tiny squares.

The only thing worse than square food, in my estimation, is square tableware. Angled plates are attractive to look at, but they are difficult to arrange, and the sharp edges are too easily chipped. Besides that, they often have square glassware to go with them. Did you ever try drinking out of a square glass? If you thought trying to drink a cup of coffee before the dentist's novocaine wore off was bad, try this sometime. It's messy.

I feel better now. I've confessed one of my idiosyncrasies relating to square things culinary. Now, of course, you may actually *like* square food, and that's perfectly all right. You just keep on enjoying those square slabs of ice cream and the wiggly cubes of Jell-O. In fact, I would be glad to save you all the little squares of carrots I find in among my frozen peas.

My own mind, however, is made up. There is no such thing as a good square meal.

On making a garage exit—
the hard way

I WASN'T going to tell you this, but since confession is good for the soul, and since there may be others out there harboring the same deep dark secret, here goes.

One morning a while back I climbed into my car, turned on the ignition, put the car in reverse and backed out of my garage.

So what, you say—people drive out of their garages all the time, don't they? Sure they do, but they have the presence of mind to *open* the garage door first!

I suppose it's too late to ask you not to laugh, especially those of you who've never committed this act—yet. I guess I can't blame you though. I myself used to chuckle a bit when I'd hear of anyone else doing it. Laughing at absent-minded souls who bomb out through garage doors is akin to whistling by the graveyard—there but by the grace of God, et cetera— so watch out.

I've learned a lot about human nature since the day my car and I "came out," so to speak. After it happens, you hover between wanting to sign yourself into some funny farm for forgetters, to chalking it up to being too busy to handle details, and laughing over it. I tended toward the latter, but with the former a very close second.

For all of you who haven't had the pleasure yet, may I offer some advice. If and when you back into your garage door without opening it, be sure to have a good alibi handy. Any excuse will help divert the attention away from your (obvious) absent-mindedness. I've heard some lulus since this happened to me. My own excuse, by the way, went like this.

On that particular morning, my boss's car was at the dealer for maintenance, so I was to give her a ride to the office.

No problem. However, the minute I stepped into the garage I remembered I hadn't cleaned out the car the night before as I'd planned. In my haste to rid the front seat of old newspapers, gum wrappers and all other disgusting telltale signs of my casual nomadic existence, I missed one very important step in my morning routine; I neglected to press the automatic door opener button.

So of course, once the front seat was cleared off, I jumped into the car, turned the key, put it into reverse and—CRASH!

Take my word for it, it's a terrible sound. You know without even turning around what has just transpired. In that one irretrievable split-second, your dignity, your self-respect and your standing in the neighborhood have just been blown to smithereens, along with your garage door.

I sat in the car projecting what my children would say if they got wind of this. "Boy, Mom's really losing it—how old was Grammy when she went senile anyway?" (They're always asking me that, as it is.)

These are the thoughts that overtake you when you do something dumb, like drive out through your garage door.

Actually, I didn't drive all the way *through* mine. When I finally dared get out of the car and assess the damage, I saw that three of the bottom panels were caved in, and one pane of glass was scattered all over the driveway. In other words, at least in good enough shape to be opened and closed with a little help.

My next step was to find some handyman-type person to repair my old door. I began at the local diner, because that's where the true network for getting things done in this town really is. On any given day there's at least one electrician, plumber, and carpenter at the counter—so how could I miss?

Well, I did. I found that *real* carpenters don't want to bother with little jobs like fixing garage doors, so after a high-level diner consultation I placed a call to my Friendly Garage Door company. It turned out that since my door was so old, replacement panels would cost me over $300, so of course they sold me a brand new door for $360.

Once installed, I noticed that there was something missing. I called my Friendly Garage Door person. "Say, I noticed that there isn't any handle on the outside of my new door."

"That's the way we do them now, lady. Nobody has handles on garage doors any more because of the automatic door openers. Besides, it's a safety feature."

Oh really, I thought. Let's just see.

I did a little research around town and elsewhere and discovered only two garage doors without any handles; one was at my house and the other belonged to the late Nicole Brown Simpson in Los Angeles. While watching the O. J. Simpson TV coverage, the camera happened to pan across the murder scene home and sure enough—no handles on her garage. So much for safety.

Needless to say, I made another call to my Friendly Garage Door Company and told them about my findings, (including the Simpsons) and they came right over the next day and installed the handle.

Now you may not believe what I'm about to tell you, but I swear it's true. Within the space of only a few weeks, not one but *three* of us in our neighborhood drove out of our garages without bothering to open the doors. I won't tell you who the other two are (the Friendly Garage Door guy knows), but I can testify that they are both of sound mind, which gives me some degree of comfort.

Since my incident, several people of varying ages have confessed to me that they too have known the agony of driving through their garage doors; some have very funny stories to tell. Two of them told of getting into their cars, hitting the "remote" button, but making the mistake of not waiting until the door was fully up before they backed out.

For some people it's not getting *out* of their garage, but getting *in* that's the problem. An antique collecting couple I know once went to an auction and after much soul-searching, they bought a beautiful, expensive 18th-century desk. After carefully strapping it onto the top of the car, they headed for home. When they turned into their driveway they remembered to hit the remote garage door opener all right, but forgot something else. CRASH! Their gorgeous antique desk never cleared the top of the garage door.

I'm thinking of starting a support group for GDTs—garage door terminators.

If any of you are brave enough to admit that you've ever done such a dastardly deed, give me a call and I'll send you a membership kit. Think of the fun we could have swapping explanations of why and how it happened. I'm sure I could get at least one follow-up column out of it. Of course, we'll have to hold the group meetings in some central location—within walking distance—just to avoid the possibility that in our haste to get there, some of us might back out through our closed garaged doors.

Let me know if you're interested. Better yet, I'll just call up my Friendly Garage Door Company. If our neighborhood is any indication, they must have quite a list by now.

Christmas shopping
á la Mrs. Kosberg

MRS. KOSBERG had two claims to fame. First, she was actress Doris Day's aunt, and second, she owned the best little lingerie shop in all of Vermont. And what Mrs. Kosberg knew how to do best (besides send yearly supplies of undies to Doris Day) was to give Class-A service to her customers.

When you bought something from Mrs. Kosberg you knew you had been waited on, as the old saying goes, hand and foot. Even before the tiny bell on the front door had stopped ringing to announce your entrance, Mrs. Kosberg was asking the magic question: "And what can I do for you today?"

Every year as I trudge through large department stores or glittery malls searching for holiday gifts, my thoughts turn longingly to the 1960's and Bennington, Vermont—and to Mrs. Kosberg. You see, shopping in her little store was almost a religious experience, and it went something like this.

"I'd like to see something in a beige slip, lace-trimmed and size 32 please." In a flash, Mrs. K. would whirl around to face a tall row of neatly stacked white boxes, scan the situation, select two or three and then place one on the spotless glass counter, square in front of her.

I loved what happened next.

She would open the box and deftly pull back each side of the crisp white tissue paper to display one beautiful beige slip, lace-trimmed and size 32. Then she would lift the delicate gossamer from its package and with the grace of a Bolshoi ballerina, twirl it high in the air until it cascaded loose from its constraining folds, then finally drape it ever so carefully over the open box and counter edge saying, "Is this what you had in mind?" Mrs. Kosberg was a pro.

It wasn't always sweetness and light in her shop, however. Whenever the Bennington College girls came in carrying ice cream cones or dill pickles, she would let them have it with both barrels. She thought nothing of telling them in no uncertain terms not to come back until their hands were empty and clean. She didn't care how much their fathers were paying to put them through school, nobody was going to drip peppermint stick ice cream or briny pickle juice on her Vanity Fairs!

I worked for Mrs. Kosberg one holiday season, and learned more about customer service in that period than I ever did before or since. She taught me how to welcome the customer, how to help without hovering, and then, how to close a deal. Mrs. K. missed her calling—today she could have made a fortune as a consultant

That individualized attention surely doesn't exist in the malls of today. Somehow those long rows of lingerie suspended from little plastic hangers, right off the Fruit-Of-The-Loom assembly line, and pawed over by hands that have been who-knows-where all day, leave a lot to be desired as far as I'm concerned. Mrs. Kosberg would turn over in her grave.

I must admit that when I first moved from the busy suburbs to a small New England town, I missed the malls for a while; I longed for their convenience and variety. Then, over the years I began to see the value of small shops once more. It is refreshing to go into a local bookstore where someone actually helps you find the book you need. Or into a clothing shop where they say "Take it home, and if you don't like it, just bring it back and we'll see what else we can do." Then there was the time I purchased a desk at a local furniture store; I asked how long it would take before it was delivered. The answer was swift: "If you're going home right now, lady, we'll just follow behind you in the truck." And they did.

How nice to find that the lost art of customer service is alive and well in some corners of the world. Welcome back, Mrs. Kosberg—I've missed you!

It's a toss-up—rickety bones
or Puberty II

RECENTLY just as my annual physical was coming to a close, my doctor brought up the "H" word.

"Hormones?" I asked. "You think I need hormones?" I knew I couldn't deny that I was aging. Just recently while standing at the bathroom sink I noticed that certain parts of my upper anatomy once visible in the mirror had now slipped down out of sight. My crows' feet had begun to beget crows' feet.

"When did you have your last period?" the doctor asked.

This question always amuses me, yet doctors insist on asking it. They must think that we women all write down in our diaries the exact date we observed the very last gasp of this female activity. I'm sorry, but I was too busy bringing up children and earning a living to make note of the occasion. Evidently I should have, however, because the medical profession seems to gauge the rest of our lives on that single event.

What started my doctor on this hormone conversation was the fact that I broke my first bone a few months before. It seems that sustaining a broken wrist is regarded by physicians as the most common first rite of passage a woman can have on the road to old age.

The next thing I knew, he was mentioning terms like bone density tests, osteoporosis and one more happy thought—dowager's hump. All kinds of scary things which, according to him, I might be able to ward off if I took hormones.

"Of course," said he, "it's your decision. Why don't you go home and think about it?"

Think about it? Believe me, I've hardly been able to think of anything else since he brought up the subject. My head's been whirling with the pros and cons of it all.

First of all, this return to hormones, or Puberty II as I call it, could open Pandora's box to who know what! For instance, will I have to go through a humiliating acne period again? I had enough heartache with that during Puberty I. Zits and wrinkles don't make for very attractive bedfellows, if you ask me. And I'll bet you anything that Medicare doesn't pay for Clearasil.

Then there's the boy-girl thing. Will I experience some sudden increased interest in the opposite sex? Will I start looking at my counter mates down at the local diner in a whole new light and start making moves on them?

Murmuring "What's your astrological sign?" Over a plateful of sunny side eggs and home fries just doesn't seem too appealing, somehow. Especially since I've spent the last few years settling into my single life, and finding precious time for my writing.

Now I suppose I'll have to chuck it all in order to launch a pursuit of the male animal. As I recall, this can be a very time consuming activity, not to mention the fact that I'll have to rethink the contents of my underwear drawer, if not the entire wardrobe.

Of course, men have it a bit easier. Sure, they may lose their hair and they might look down one day to discover that their belt buckles have dropped out of sight forever, but their hormones don't bail out suddenly the way ours do. We women are the ones with the big dilemmas to face.

And speaking of dilemmas—I'll have to call my doctor soon with my decision. I'm leaning toward the hormone therapy. Too bad, in a way, because after all these years I'd finally gotten used to hot flashes!

Shopping for a one-holer

I'LL BET my friend and I must have trekked through three different shopping malls before we finally found me a one-holer. They're not easy to come by now, you know. I guess today's shoppers prefer the more modern versions, but give me the old fashioned kind any day.

I was getting desperate to find one because you see, one's need for a one-holer increases with one's age, especially for women.

Now, just so you don't misunderstand me here, when I say *one-holer* I mean a pocketbook—or purse—which has only one major compartment in it. You see, today's versions are just the opposite—crammed with sections for credit cards, eyeglasses, checkbooks, pens, gloves. You name it and they've got a place to put it.

I happen to think, however, that life today has enough decisions as it is, without having to figure out where to put your sunglasses or that half-eaten Snickers Bar you want to save till later. When I'm in a hurry and have to conduct an all-out search through endless compartments before I find my checkbook, this is the last straw.

I have friends who just love this type of pocketbook. They say they'd much rather rummage through those little cubbyholes than dig down deep into the cavernous insides of a one-holer. I say that with *their* kind of purse you could spend all day looking, and never come up with your Rolaids.

Did you ever stand in line at the grocery store while some lady ahead of you began looking for a pen in one of those multiple hole purses? Take my word for it—get in line behind a one-holer person and you'll get home for dinner a lot faster.

One year my daughter gave me one of those organizer purses. It's not much bigger than a paperback book, and genuine leather, too. But on close examination I found that the thing had compartments for my credit cards, checkbook, calculator, change, bills, monthly planner, address book, mirror, glasses and pens! Ten separate places for me to investigate on my way to my dental floss.

Suddenly my daughter looked at me and said "On second thought, it might be too confusing for you."

Now THAT hurt! I like to think I'm still a viable, functioning person, but on the other hand, no one knows us the way our kids do. My daughter knew how happy I was to swap a house for a condominium and a full time job for a part time one. And we both knew that one of my new goals in life was to simplify, simplify, simplify—including purses.

Since it takes me longer to retrieve things these days—including pertinent data in my brain—I say let's leave those multiple compartment purses to the Baby Boomer and X generations. On them they look good. They can still remember where they put what. But for those of us who are old enough to remember World War II, poodle skirts and when Dick Clark really *did* have brown hair, it's time to simplify.

It's time to bring back the one-holer!

Patrolling smut on the net

NOW THAT computers are becoming standard equipment in most American homes, parents are having a difficult time deciding what their children should and should not see on the Internet. The pros and cons of censorship have been argued all the way from small town barber shops to the Halls of Congress in Washington.

My first reaction to this dilemma is to reject the idea of censorship on Constitutional grounds. But then, I don't have any young fry in my house telephoning those 1-900 sex hotlines, or typing in dirty words on the Internet chat lines.

Curious about what kids are actually seeing on the Net these days, I decided to find out for myself. A smut committee of one, so to speak. So the other night I logged on to my computer, fired up the Internet and clicked on a square that said 'Net Search'. It was time to type in the subject I wanted to look up—so I took off my adult's hat and tried to think as a ten or eleven year old.

What would a prepubescent, sweaty-but-not-yet-using-deodorant, hat-on-backwards kid of today be looking up, anyway?

Let's say there's a group of boys (it's not that girls don't do the same thing, but for the sake of argument, let's assume they are male) and it's raining out so they can't play ball, they've seen the local movies and the tv shows are all summer re-runs. Given this scenario, someone suddenly says—"Hey! Let's look up something on the Net!"

"How about girls!" someone suggests. Now, keep in mind that this is the age group that barely acknowledges the presence of females in public, but that doesn't mean they aren't curious about them when nobody is looking. So off they go to the house with the best computer and fastest modem and log on.

Let's see now, what words do you suppose they'd be apt to type into this square that says 'net search'? I made an executive decision and took a chance that the subject they'd enter just might begin with the word 'naked'. So I typed in *n-a-k-e-d w-o-m-e-n* and sat back to see what happened next.

Well, plenty happened. First, an amazing statistic flashed on the screen telling me how many choices or sites on this topic are available in this computer of mine. Are you ready? 1,896,749—and something told me there wasn't going to be a Renoir or Titian painting among them.

Now let's get this into perspective. How many sites of ANYTHING are on the web, anyway?

If the boys looked up chocolate chip cookies, for instance, they'd find there were 90,082 sites. Baseball—284,029. We're getting closer, but those naked ladies (or any of the sites that fall under the category of sex) have them all beat.

With these fascinating statistics behind me, I commenced my research project. After a little whirring and clicking, up on the screen popped a series of titles and descriptions of the various sites or articles about the topic. The first one was enough to curl my hair. The written descriptions bore no resemblance to the ones in my town library's card catalog.

I hadn't seen so many of those words on one page since my son took that sex education course when he was 11. One evening, part way through that session, we parents were invited to attend without our children. The instructors passed out newsprint and magic markers and told us to write down every sexual and/or anatomical slang word we could think of.

When we finished squirming and scribbling, the lists were taped up on the walls. It was like a crash course in locker room graffiti. Though I was in my early forties, I'd never even heard of some of those terms. Then came the shocker. "You will be interested to know," said the instructor, "that there isn't a word up here that your children didn't write down for us when we did this exercise with them!"

So I figured that if the kids 20 years ago weren't surprised by these words, they surely wouldn't be today, so I resumed my computer experiment and clicked on the first title.

WARNING, the screen said. IF YOU ARE NOT 18 YEARS OF AGE OR OVER YOU MAY NOT SEE THIS SECTION.

Oh *sure,* I thought. Do you suppose my imaginary kids would be scared off by that admonishment? Not too likely. Besides, who'd enforce it?

So I did what the kids would do—clicked on a square called "HOT FREE ADULT PICS ."

The first photo came on the screen . They were naked, all right. There were men and women in the color photo in poses that surely didn't lend themselves to playing Scrabble or reading *The Times.*

At this point, I decided to do the only thing a self respecting grandmother of four could do. I got up and pulled down the window shades. I figured that I might have a difficult time convincing my neighbors that these images on my screen came under the heading of research.

The stuff went from bad to worse, depending on your point of view. There was nothing left to the imagination. Although not every model was completely naked (some were wearing high heeled shoes) it was a far cry from when I was growing up and sneaking peeks at those jungle pictures in the National Geographic.

After seeing more flesh than I care to see in a lifetime, I turned off the computer and thought about how this may or may not affect young children. This, along with the chat lines in which young girls and boys write in to say how lonely they are, and the pay-per-look pornography that could wipe out the kids' allowances in five minutes, gave me pause to wonder where this will all lead.

My guess is that for most kids, the rain will stop, the ball game will resume, a new movie will come to the local theater, and their lives will go on as usual. Still, I don't envy the parents who will surely have to keep a wary eye on Internet temptations of the future.

Sometimes being in the grandparent era has its advantages. What we do or watch is pretty much up to us. Think of it. Why, we could even log onto the Internet and search for n-a-k-e-d O-L-D *w-o-m-e-n*, and no one would care!

P.S. For your information, there are over 2 million naked old women sites on the web. One can only assume that many of them are scientific in nature and have to do with the effects of gravity on the human body.

There's a small hotel . . .

IT WAS a dark and rainy afternoon this fall, tailor-made weather for what I had on my agenda.

I was in Durham, NH, for the weekend to do some writing, because I'd discovered that for some reason the New England Center's hotel, the Adams Tower, is a very fertile place for my brain to wax creative. I often can get more ideas developed and pages written there than almost anywhere.

The tower is an angular building centered in a patch of woods so tall and thick that the morning sun has to fight its way through to let you know it's daybreak.

Each room has a wall of floor-to-ceiling windows, also built on an angle, with a desk or writing table centered in front of it. The only view is of the woods which wrap around your window separating you from the outside world.

Anyway, on this particular rainy afternoon, I was standing in the lobby waiting for the elevator when suddenly the doors opened and two children burst out almost knocking me over. They were probably no older than 10, and laughing and giggling and having a wonderful time playing elevator games, and exploring the hotel in general.

No sooner did they get out of one car when they were on to the next, pushing buttons so that they could stop at all eight floors. They had created a youthful oasis of fun in an otherwise quiet and staid hotel on a rainy afternoon.

I always knew that hotels could be marvelous playgrounds for bored youngsters. They are places just waiting for mischief to happen. Shades of little Eloise, that fictitious but precocious character who lived and cavorted in the grownup world of the upscale Plaza Hotel.

Later that afternoon, in my room, I wasn't making much headway with my writing projects because the children had reminded me that I had some hotel memories of my own—and I began to revisit them in my mind.

When I was about 11, a family friend purchased a small hotel and asked my mother whether she'd come down to cook and manage the kitchen for a month or so, just to help him out. Although she hadn't worked outside the home in years, she said yes, "just for a month or so."

The month or so turned out to be 20 years, and over that time, we all learned a great deal about hotels in general and that one in particular. I loved every minute of it.

I loved the days when I'd stop in at the hotel after school and visit my mother's kitchen for a little nourishment. Sometimes, I'd sit out in the dining room with my apple pie and milk and make believe I was a paying guest. Other times I'd curl up on a couch in the lobby watching the guests come and go. This was a small hotel, mind you—no Ritz Carlton this—but for a youngster it had its share of excitement and intrigue.

One winter—the last year we were to live out in the country—my father decided he couldn't face shoveling our long driveway another time, so the three of us moved into the hotel until spring. My mother and father's room was on the second floor and my single room was on the third.

Now this was quite a worldly living arrangement for a 13-year-old girl. I supposed that I was probably the only one in the whole junior high school who was living in a hotel.

By six o'clock each morning, my mother was at work in the hotel kitchen, so my father and I would eat breakfast together—he with his *Boston Post* and I with my last-minute homework. Because it was before the dining room officially opened, we often ate breakfast in the lounge, sitting right up at the bar on high stools.

Now I was *sure* I was the only one in the whole school who started her day looking up at rows and rows of liquor bottles and tall stemmed glasses.

One day, this new-found sense of independence caused me to do something I'd never done before—skip school. In her off time, my mother was an avid reader and always had two or three library books at the ready. On a particular afternoon, I was visiting my parents' second-floor room and for lack of anything else to do, started leafing through the books. It soon became apparent that one of them, Somerset Maugham's *The Razor's Edge*, had situations in it that didn't appear in our junior high curriculum.

By today's standards, it was probably pretty innocent language, but to me this was the most sensational thing to come our way since *Lady Chatterly's Lover*. The only time I could read this book was when my mother was working, and that meant skipping school. When you live in a hotel and your mother is down in the kitchen all day, this can be a challenge, but the next day I took it on.

I had my breakfast in the bar with Dad as usual, picked up my lunch bag in the kitchen from my mother, and off—or up—I went. I hid out all day in my third-story room, reading what I considered to be torrid page after torrid page.

For someone as shy and retiring as I was then, this was a pretty exciting day, and unless the chambermaid told her, I don't think my mother ever found out.

When I was a little older, my mother and I would take an occasional trip to Boston for an overnight, just the two of us. We'd ride down on the bus and stay at the Hotel Touraine at the corner of Tremont and Boylston Streets. It was rather Spartan and a far cry from the Ritz Carlton, but it was what we could afford.

I remember we would unpack our things, then stand at the window like two out-of-state neophytes that we were, in awe of the busy intersection and Boston Common down below.

Since my mother's livelihood and interest revolved around food, we would always splurge by going up to the Parker House or to the Sheraton Plaza for lunch to try their cuisine and to get ideas. Then we would sit in their lobbies awhile to watch what my mother used to call "the other half" go by.

And in the evenings back at the Touraine, I can still hear

her insisting that I fill the tub and take a bath. "After all," she'd say, "we're *paying* for it!"

Most of us don't spend much time in hotels these days. As a matter of fact, there aren't many of them left. With the exception of those owned by the Donald Trumps and Leona Helmsleys of this world, most of the grand hotels are kept alive only through novels and old films. By and large, they have been replaced by egg crate-like buildings called motels, which are efficient, but to my mind not nearly so social or interesting.

All this hotel talk reminds me that it's time to revisit Durham again. Maybe this time I won't get sidetracked with my own reminiscences and actually get some work done. Then when I'm finished, I just might go a few extra floors on that elevator—just for old times' sake.

II. We Mortals Are Courageous

"Man is harder than iron,
stronger than stone;
and more fragile than a rose."
—*Turkish Proverb*

Alice doesn't live here anymore

I REMEMBER the day I first met her. My future husband and I were on our way to his home town and the bus had barely left Boston's Park Square station when he blurted out, "I'd better tell you about my mother."

I could tell by his tone that I should pay attention to what he was going to tell me.

"My mother doesn't wear any makeup, she has no style, and her stockings hang down around her ankles in little rolls."

I supposed he was telling me this because I did wear some makeup and had some interest in fashion—as did my own mother—but that surely didn't mean that I thought all women had to do likewise.

"And she doesn't *do* anything!"

He explained that his mother had given birth to seven children and since her husband was away in the military part of that time, she felt she had done her duty as far as working around the house was concerned. So, she sat and she read books and magazines, period.

My curiosity grew with every passing mile. What kind of a woman was this, anyway?

When we arrived at the house we were greeted by "The Colonel," as he was called, and it was easy to see that my future husband got his warmth and gregariousness from his father. This man definitely played the starring role in the family, but it was the supporting actress I was anxious to meet.

Alice Johnson Duncanson was sitting on the sofa when we entered the house. She was a smiling woman with ocean blue eyes, a shock of greying, untamable hair and plump cheeks that were naturally pink without any assistance from Max Factor or Revlon—just as I'd been told.

I don't recall the details of her clothing but I cannot forget her shoes—they were the sturdy black lace-up type with wide solid heels—strong enough to hold up a woman twice her size. Of course, I tried not to stare at her ankles for fear she'd suspect I was looking at those small rings of excess nylon.

That was over 30 years ago. This week we buried Alice Johnson Duncanson at the age of 91, and her funeral didn't do her justice.

I suppose it wasn't the minister's fault; he was brought in from another town on short notice, and except for viewing her in the casket, had never laid eyes on Alice before. He led us through the usual comforting scriptural passages with feeling, but it was obvious from his perfunctory reading of her vital statistics made available by the funeral director, that he preferred this to reading any of the human interest items lovingly written by a family member and given to him

So in a matter of about 15 minutes, all those years as a daughter, wife, mother, grandmother and great-grandmother were quietly dismissed, almost as if they'd never existed.

On the long ride home after the funeral I reflected on Mom and I began thinking of how she surprised us all. None of us would have predicted her living so long. After all, her siblings were long deceased, and remember—she had her seven children and then rested—no exercise, no traveling and not many interests to fill the years.

But despite the fact that she was regarded by her neighbors as reclusive early on, Alice commenced to evolve somewhere along the way.

After the Colonel died, a slow but sure metamorphosis began taking shape. She started to say yes to things she had refused for years. Take riding in the Memorial Day parade with the other Gold Star Mothers, for instance. Her husband had been the grand marshal of that parade for years and could never get her to take part in it. Suddenly, however, there was Alice Duncanson riding down the street in one of those open cars . . . and we all watched from the sidelines with surprise and pride.

As the years went by and her heart grew weaker and her

eyesight worsened, her mind never lost a single cell. When the family would play Trivial Pursuit at holiday time, everyone wanted Alice on their team because even though she might doze off occasionally, she could always be counted on to wake up in time to come up with the answer, and she was never wrong.

Outwardly she was quiet and preferred to listen when in a crowd, but inwardly she was a very strong woman. She dealt with losses better than anyone I know. Her first test was losing a three year old daughter to pneumonia. Later, her oldest son's plane went down in the Bermuda Triangle, never to be recovered.

Then there were the heart attacks—all swift and fatal. First her husband and then her second son, my husband, in his mid forties, followed by her youngest son a few years later. Through all of this her demeanor never changed. Life went on—there was no room for self-pity. That's the way she was, and how I admired her for it.

The role of matriarch turned out to be one of her finest. She was proud of us all and became our most reliable sources of family news, keeping everyone informed.

Alice was born, raised and spent 88 of her 91 years in the same house. It will soon be time for her three remaining children to begin going through the remnants of three generations' worth of living in the old place. It won't be easy.

After the funeral, I drove past the house on my way out of town, and I couldn't help thinking that my husband was right about two things: his mother never wore makeup and her stockings did indeed always seem to hang down around her ankles in little rolls. But he was wrong when he said she didn't have style and never did anything, because the older she grew, the more evident her own unique style became. What she did best was to be there for us all.

I have no regrets about my relationship with this woman and by her own admission, 91 years is plenty long enough to be on this earth. Still, I am going to miss her.

My world will never be quite the same now because as of last Thursday morning, Alice doesn't live here anymore.

From rhubarb to roses

I GOT thinking the other day about all the views I've had from my various office windows over the years and decided that the one I have now is the best of all. Especially in the springtime. You see, from my desk I can look out at Mildred McLaughlin's yard—and it's turned out to be a bonus I never expected; partly due, I suppose, to the 200 year-old house, partly to Mildred herself, and partly to the ever changing yard.

The house is a small, what I call shy, house because it doesn't face the street. It is tucked in sideways and wrapped around tightly by a church, a busy state highway, an apartment house and a parking lot. The upper story has a series of little shuttered windows set so low to the floor that I imagine tiny creatures from Mary Norton's book ,"The Borrowers," are living there.

Mildred has lived in this house for 65 of her 90 years—a record hard to come by these days. This is where she and her late husband raised their children, and where she continues to keep a busy daily routine. So much so that her family has placed a large sign up over her sink which reads, SLOW DOWN, as a friendly reminder.

But it's the yard that comes into focus outside my office window—and it's become fascinating to observe the seasons coming and going there.

It begins with the rhubarb in the spring, pushing its way out of the cold ground while many other plants are still sleeping. Although the lilac tree will soon bloom and garner all the attention of passers by, it's the rhubarb that comes first, and stays for a good long time. It's not as photogenic as the lilac but it produces a crop steady enough to assure Mildred of makings for rhubarb pies and cakes all summer long.

Then, no sooner do a few stray daffodils and tulips burst forth and the geraniums get set-in near the side door, when it's time for Mildred to plant the vegetable garden. It is a small one—just big enough for a few hills of tomatoes, squash, beets, beans and carrots, which eventually find their way onto Mildred's dining room table. Last year a row of gorgeous double pink poppies suddenly sprang up and positioned themselves along the little fence surrounding the garden.

"I have no idea how they got there," mused Mildred. "Probably blew in on the wind—but aren't they pretty."

The real stars of Mildred's back yard, however, are her roses. There are two stands of them. One is a row of wild roses hugging the back wall of the old garage. Though beautiful, these are the low maintenance variety; they would probably come up and flourish whether Mildred paid them any mind or not. Not so for the other stand. These are the cultivated roses, many of which have been blooming under her care for 25 years. They are brilliant in color, delicate in design and cared for as if they were Mildred's own flesh and blood. I often see her out there early in the morning tending to them with her clippers, bug repellant, and just plain TLC.

Last year she was not a bit happy with their growth because there was no spring to speak of. Where they usually stand as tall as Mildred herself, they were a foot or so shorter, but breathtaking just the same. Once in a while, Mildred would bring me over a particularly handsome blossom to put on my desk. Another bonus I never dreamed of.

In the Fall, the tiny blue and purple asters creep in around the edges of the yard as a signal to the others that it's time to go. The days become numbered for the geraniums near Mildred's side door and the large rhubarb leaves finally turn brown on the edges and hang low to the ground. Her roses are the last to go. Sometimes it is well into October before Mildred cuts them back and lovingly puts them to bed by covering them with a blanket of pine needles for their winter's sleep.

But now comes Spring, the best season of all. It's time for Mildred McLaughlin's back yard to come alive again and it surely will. I know this is true because this morning I saw the rhubarb leaves just beginning to make their annual appearance. And as Mildred McLaughlin herself says, once the rhubarb comes, can roses be far behind?

The end of the movie

THEY HAD all left for the funeral so the house was empty, except for little Andrew and myself. Although I wished I could have gone with them, my job was to stay home with my grandson. It seemed the very least I could do; after all, he was her grandson, too.

When I arrived at the house a half hour earlier, they were all there in the living room—husband, daughter, son, and spouses—all of them still in their casual clothes. They were reluctant to get changed into the things they'd chosen to wear that day, for once they were dressed, that would mean they were ready to leave.

There were the uneasy remarks about whether the dark suits would fit, and the appropriateness of the dress that hadn't been worn in so long. There was the nervous good natured banter about who had eaten the most from the large plate of cookies that shared the dining room table with an overflowing box of sympathy notes and cards. All elements of conversation that help us survive such times.

Finally, one by one, they filed upstairs to change, and within a few minutes they were on their way to the services.

The house was so quiet after they'd gone. Even Andrew had been put down for a nap in a portable crib up in the spare bedroom. He, of course, was too young to grasp the significance of this day. For all he knew, things were quite normal in this house. His mom and dad had gotten him up, dressed and fed him as usual this morning while engaging in conversation with him that only parents of an 18-month-old could understand.

Andrew's little life still had its momentum and routine. The word 'funeral' wasn't in his vocabulary yet.

It had snowed the night before and the bright sun reflected back through the windows, accenting everything in the house that had her touch on it. The photos on the stereo, the color scheme, the placement of the furniture, the dishes set out on the hutch—it struck me then just how much of herself a woman brings to a home. It's not that men don't leave their mark on the nest, but traditionally, it's the women who seem most naturally disposed to turning houses into homes. Even busy women like Lena.

I could tell just from the years I'd known her that this house wasn't built or decorated without detailed planning. Lena loved to plan. Whether it was her teaching sessions for her class at the high school or deciding what brand of microwave oven to buy, she researched and planned and planned and researched. The newspapers were thoroughly scanned, the pages in The Consumer's Guide were well-worn, and occasionally she'd call a family member to let them know that an item they'd been searching for was on sale, and that this would be the time to buy. Her penchant for preparation served her family and friends well.

Even in the last months of her life, she was still planning. The house would eventually be sold, so it should have new, more modern windows and other upgrading. Plans were drawn up, and sure enough, not long ago the house took on a fresher, more up-to-date look so that it would appeal to some future buyer when it came time to sell.

A terminal illness, however, is no respecter of plans. It never seems to care that you have things left to do in your life, and in Lena's case a chance to enjoy some well-earned retirement with her husband.

I never knew anyone to write a word like 'cancer' into their long or short-term goals, but I could think of many who, once afflicted, handled it amazingly well. They gave credence to the old adage that hangs by my kitchen sink which says "If life gives you lemons, make lemonade." Lena knew how to make lemonade.

First, she sought the best medical attention she could find, and then she determined that the rest was up to her. Her theme song was never "poor me," although no one would have blamed her if it were. She took a fresh look at the rest of her life and made the most of it, month by month and day by day.

As I sat there on her living room couch in front of her shiny new windows, I was revisited by a recurring memory of my freshman year at college. The rule at that time was that all female freshmen had to be in their dormitories by 7 p.m. or face the wrath of the Women's Judiciary Board. Besides being grossly unfair, since male students had no such rule, it also meant that when we went to the local theater we always had to jump up and run back to the dorm without knowing how the film turned out. We never got to see the end of the movie.

Now Lena wouldn't get to see the end of the movie as far as her family and friends' lives were concerned, including little Andrew and his cousins Shannon and Stephen. But then I thought, neither would I. Or anyone else for that matter.

By design and for the continuity of life itself, all our movie reels are set into motion at different times, and play for varying lengths of time. Maybe, I thought, this is something we should remind ourselves of every so often, if only to ensure that we make the most of the scripts in our own movies while we are here.

Soon, noises began emanating from the upstairs spare room signaling the end of a nap. I brought Andrew down and settled myself on the living room floor to watch him play with his father's old matchbox cars that had been carefully stored away all these years by his Grandma Lena.

Looking at him, there was little question where he got that shining dark hair or the distinct bow shaped mouth, and from some of his early precise habits, I wouldn't even be surprised if he turned out to be a planner, too.

The sun was going down and I knew it wouldn't be long before cars pulled into the driveway. As I built and rebuilt makeshift bridges and roads for the old miniature trucks and cars, I found myself wanting to say one last thing to Andrew before the others arrived home. I was bound I'd say it even though I knew he wouldn't understand a word of it.

Listen young man, I said, I may not be able to be around

to see the end of the movie as far as your life's journey is concerned, but you can bet that for as long as I'm here, I don't intend to take my eyes off the movie screen for a single minute.

I learned this lesson from someone very special—your Grandma Lena.

Dealing with a very pressing problem

WE WOMEN have finally gotten the message out that even though breast cancer lags behind heart disease when it comes to the actual number who die every year, it still has us plenty worried. So much so that the number of us who take advantage of a diagnostic tool like the mammogram is increasing each year.

Not that we all enjoy going in for this procedure; it's not exactly a walk in the park. I'll never forget the very first one I had. I was in my forties and my doctor wanted me to have what they call a 'baseline' x-ray, against which they would compare all subsequent films for changes. It was administered by a woman who definitely missed her calling. She should have been Nurse Ratchett in the movie *One Flew Over the Cuckoo's Nest*, or perhaps a commander leading a SWAT team to annihilate the Ayatollah.

She was a flat chested woman who seemed to have it in for any female who had even a remotely discernable breast. "Come on, you might as well get it over with!" said she. As her rough hands arranged parts of my anatomy on the apparatus, it became clear to me that she must have a night job fixing Hondas.

When she brought down the heavy glass plates I thought I was done for. Seconds seemed like years. In fact, I thought she either misplaced the release button or was trying to kill me, or both. For a while there, it appeared that she'd gone out for lunch, leaving me frozen in a position you wouldn't wish on your worst enemy. I had visions of myself fainting, dangling from the machine until she finished her coffee and dessert. When she finally did set me free she said, "See, I told you it wouldn't hurt!" It was obvious this woman never had a mammogram herself.

As I recall that was the only time I ever wrote to a hospital to complain. I simply told them there are people cut out for that sensitive job and then there are others like this Nurse Ratchett who, if they even came near the place should set off an alarm to alert every woman in hearing distance to stay away. I noticed that the next time I went for a mammogram, she was nowhere in sight.

They have come a long way in this field. The surroundings are much more "woman-friendly," pleasant and less clinical. The technicians are better trained, too; they now deal compassionately with women who are uncomfortable with the procedure and understandably afraid of what the x-rays could show.

My local hospital used to have a little sign on the wall next to the mammography equipment which read, "We Compress because we Care." I notice that it's not around any more either. I guess they finally figured out that even looking at the word "compress" causes referred pain

I enjoy being a woman. No offense to the men but we women have an unspoken sisterhood that is hard to match. Whether it's the shared pain of childbirth, the sorrow of bereavement or just the ability to go out to lunch together and tell it like it is, we feed off each other and we grow. Of course, one other thing we share is a concern about developing breast cancer. We've seen the statistics; we can count. Hopefully this worry may someday be only a fading memory.

Even the recollections of Nurse Ratchett may soften in time; hope springs eternal.

Requiem for a gas station

I was driving through the town I once called home not long ago and dropped in at Norman and Edna's donut shop, for old times' sake.

As we caught up on each other's lives over a cup of Edna's coffee, it didn't take long for our conversation to get around to Phil Levine's Mobil Station and the day they tore the place down.

I remembered that when the wrecking crew showed up that morning, all of us regulars at the counter peered out the window over our coffee cups, toward the lot next door as we waited for a slice of our past to disappear.

We all agreed that there was no need in God's world for all that big equipment they brought in to do the job. Shoot, the place had stood empty for a couple of years at that point, so a good huff and puff by the bulldozer operator could have blown the thing down in no time.

It was a sad day for us all. We weren't ashamed to admit that over the years, that rattletrap of a garage had crept into the hearts of all of us, because Phil Levine's Mobil Station was a garage with a difference.

First of all, it had to be the dirtiest station in town. This was no place for sissies or anyone who wanted to just play at being a mechanic. Real work went on here, and work meant dirt!

A friend and I used to have a running battle about whose service station (as in Full Serve) was the best. She was always bragging that her garage in upscale Wellesley was so fancy that the mechanics all wore white coveralls. Of course, she *had* me there.

I couldn't exactly picture white coveralls at Phil Levine's. When you were brave enough to make your way through the dank, cold bowels of Phil's place, you could barely make out the mechanics because they were always dressed in deep greens and browns to match the grease. Fixing cars was their thing—not fashion.

The mechanics' apparel wasn't the only thing that was dirty at the old station—the language was too. My clergyman husband loved that garage and was the unofficial chaplain of what he called "The Levine Chapel."

He used to say it was ecumenical through and through, since there was always at least one Catholic, Protestant and Jew working there at any given time to keep the discussions on religion lively—and every one of them an expert, according to them.

"And," as my husband used to put it, "the Lord's name gets mentioned there with the same regularity as it does in church." And that was no lie. Every time a tire iron dropped or a jack slipped, the Deity's name got invoked loud and clear.

As a matter of fact, the garage vocabulary was rather extensive. The Reverend used to say that it was the only place in town that made him feel as if he were back in the Navy again. It gave him the chance to use words he didn't have occasion to utter too often around the parish.

And, of course, he never missed the Christmas parties. Everyone who was *anyone* was there. People you'd least expect would sit around in the grease and fumes and eat holiday goodies, and drink holiday cheer at all hours during the holiday season.

Christmas may not have been Phil's holiday but he sure knew how to celebrate it. From the amount of liquid cheer that was ingested at those parties, everyone knew it was never a good idea to schedule your car for repair at Levine's on Christmas week.

When you drove in to get gas there, you soon learned that Phil's guys dispensed a lot more than mere octane. While your tank was filling and you were a captive audience in your car, you would get an earful of advice on everything under the sun, whether you wanted it or not. You name it, and they'd have an opinion on it.

They knew the "real scoop" on the Kennedy assassination, and what we should have done with the Vietnam War, and the absolute best place to put our money so the government wouldn't get it, et cetera.

And if you disagreed with them, forget it. By the time they'd finished their expounding, the tank would be filled, you'd have your change, and these graduates of the Phil Levine Charm School would be on to their next victim.

Phil Levine was a blustery, hardworking, hands-on type of owner. He was in business to make a living just like the next guy, but if you went in to buy new tires and he felt yours still had some life in them, he'd tell you so.

Or, if he knew you were hard-pressed for money, he'd look around the garage to find you some used ones to "tide you over" until you could afford the new ones.

He was tough on the outside but had a heart of gold on the inside.

I'll never forget the first time I drove the family station wagon up to the old Mobil pumps after my husband died. It was then that I realized just how much our family had identified with this crazy, frenetic, run-down place.

Phil himself came out to the car and I remember saying to him through the tears, "But Phil, I've never had to buy gas for a car before—I don't know whether to ask for so many dollars' worth or so many gallons. I don't know *anything* about what makes a car run!"

Phil just put his big grease-stained hand on my arm and said the magic words: "For crying out loud, Joann, just leave the worrying about the car to us, will yah? And as far as your not knowing anything about cars, I've got news for you—neither did your husband. As a matter of fact, damn few of my customers do—male *or* female!"

My car received excellent service for several years after that conversation, until finally the time came when health reasons forced Phil to give up the station and move south.

A couple of guys tried to keep it going for awhile, but it just wasn't the same somehow. After two years, they slammed down the doors of the repair bays for the last time and it was all over. The place had done its duty. It didn't owe anybody anything.

So, watching it being torn down that day wasn't easy. And seeing the overgrown lot still vacant the other day wasn't easy either.

I miss that old place, and the motley crew who ran it. I even miss the blue language and the unsolicited advice.

Rest in peace, Phil Levine's Mobil Station.

Rub-a-dub-dub—a shower or tub?

I HAVE a friend who says she can't understand why people take baths. Not that she's dirty or suffers from hydrophobia—far from it—it's just that she is a shower person as opposed to a tub person.

Her rationale is that when we bathe in a tub, we wash off all the dirt and grime of the day, and that is good; but then we sit there in the same water that has just taken on all those impurities, and rewash ourselves with it. And that, according to my friend, *isn't* good.

This shower-vs.-tub debate has gone on for years. There's a whole segment of bathers out there who wouldn't dream of bothering to fill up a tub to loll around in it for any length of time. They'd rather turn on that shower, jump in, get clean and refreshed, and jump out.

Some of us, on the other hand, happen to think that tub baths border on being sacred. They provide a time of relaxation and renewal and a place to escape the cares of the day. A sort of therapy with faucets.

It wouldn't at all surprise me, for instance, to find that the poet Wordsworth wrote his famous lines about the world being "too much with us" while basking in a tub somewhere trying to get away from it all. I can't see how a shower would have fostered anything so profound.

And what would Jane Austen and her crowd have done without those sojourns to the English city of Bath? Going to Bath (rhyming, of course, with "moth") for the British literary greats was socially the thing to do. Evidently, soaking in those underground mineral springs was very conducive to conversation.

I suspect if they'd all been closeted in some shower stalls all day instead, the literature of that period might not have been so prolific, and the likes of *Pride and Prejudice* might never have seen the light of day.

Although there are still a few people around today who avail themselves of spas, the rest of us are happy to settle for a tub surrounded with walls of fiberglass, or worse yet, innumerable squares of ceramic tile held together by grout that insists on turning black when we're not looking.

We Americans are so spoiled. We take things like showers, tubs, and seemingly endless hot water for granted. We carry the "cleanliness is next to Godliness" adage to the extreme, and waste billions of gallons of water in the process.

It wasn't that long ago when entire households had to share the same bath water. The name of the game was to get at the head of the line—for very obvious reasons. Maybe we ought to revive this custom to help conserve one of our natural resources.

I know I said earlier that shower people jump in and out of showers and don't linger. But that isn't always true and anyone who's ever had a teenager in the family knows it.

I found this out when my son first discovered girls. Literally overnight, this person who had to be reminded and reminded to get himself cleaned up, began taking up squatters' rights in the shower, lathering up all the soap he could get his hands on. Even though the water and electric bills went up, I always felt I owed these girls a debt of gratitude.

Since we're talking here about bathing, I probably should tell you about what happened to Mrs. Loker. She was an elderly friend of my mother who lived over in the next town in a farmhouse, which by anyone's standards was rustic.

The place had no bath tub or shower, a deprivation my mother could never have endured. Although Mrs. Loker always appeared to be neat and clean, my mother felt it a shame that she would never know the pleasure of immersing herself in a tub filled with warm, soothing, sudsy water.

One day during one of Mrs. Loker's visits, my mother threw caution to the wind and asked her outright whether she would like to take a bath before she went home. My mother didn't know what possessed her to ask, but lo and behold, didn't Mrs. Loker allow as how she would like to take my mother up on her offer.

Since our friend was in her 80s and rather frail, my mother gave her some initial assistance, and then left her there to soak away to her heart's content for quite a long time. I suppose the combination of the warm, fragrant water and the afternoon sunlight streaming into the room, made for a very pleasant and unusual interlude for our friend. When she left, she thanked my mother profusely for the experience.

The story doesn't end there. The next morning, my mother got a call from Mrs. Loker's son, and the news wasn't good. His mother had passed away in the night. Just like that, he said, she went in her sleep.

My mother was mortified. She was sure that she was the cause of her little friend's death, and that climbing in and out of the tub and soaking in that warm water was just too much of a shock to her system.

For years after that, whenever Mrs. Loker's name came up in conversation, mother would be revisited by feelings of guilt.

I was very young when this all happened, but over the years, as my tub fills slowly and the scent of perfumed soap begins to trail out into the other rooms of the house, I sometimes think of my mother and her elderly friend and the day of "the bath."

I've come to the conclusion that Mrs. Loker probably had herself a perfectly glorious afternoon that day, immersed in warm, cleansing water for the first time in years.

In fact, I'd like to think that when the end came, she was not only at peace when she met her Maker, but thanks to my mother, this nice little lady was absolutely *squeaky clean* when she went to her reward!

Two men, two lives,
but just one ocean

THIS is a tale of two men. First, Dave.

I arrived at work one morning just in time to hear him in the next office, moaning and groaning. I rushed in.

"Are you sick?" I asked.

"No," he shot back, "but I haven't got long to live!"

He proceeded to show me a promotional piece he'd just received in the mail. It was a gadget that calculated the number of years a person has left on earth by utilizing criteria such as weight, height, age, family history, and eating habits.

"According to this, I've only got about 32 years to go! This is terrible!" he exclaimed.

Dave, barely into his 40's, had just had a glimpse of what it's like to discover that you are on the downhill side of the slippery slope of longevity. Actuarially speaking, he just might have fewer years *ahead* of him than *behind*! A sobering thought even for someone like Dave who was the comedian of our office, capable of cheering us all up just by entering the room.

Since I had a lot less tread left on my tires than he did, I couldn't offer "old" Dave much consolation. I'd be lucky if I had half as many years left as this healthy basketball playing, mountain climbing, motorcycle riding Baby Boomer had!

Now for the second man, Morris Schwartz.

Chances are you never heard of Morris (or Morrie) Schwartz. I hadn't either until I happened to read a newspaper article about him, and then caught him being interviewed on TV's "Nightline" program.

Like our friend Dave, Morrie Schwartz is also looking at the years he has left on earth. In his case, however, the span remaining is very short; he is suffering from Lou Gehrig's

Disease and is becoming more debilitated by the day—and the clock is running

This 79 year old Brandeis University professor has joined the growing number of terminally ill patients who choose not to withdraw from the world, but to remain open and connected. They share their feelings with others while traversing the medical mine fields of their last days and months. Not all of them do it well, but this man does.

Morrie Schwartz tells it like it is—no Pollyanna platitudes—there's no time for that. He describes in detail what it is like to live with a disease that leaves your mind intact while it whittles away at your muscle and sinew. He tells about the good times and the bad and admits to not knowing what, if anything, is ahead of him after death.

This man is not just sitting around watching sunsets and listening to Mozart, however; he is instead thinking about attending his own funeral. He plans to gather friends and family to share memories of the good times, to reminisce, to laugh and cry together while he is still able to do so.

In his *Reflections on Maintaining One's Composure With a Fatal Illness*, he offers words not only to die by, but to live by. "Accept the past without denying it or discarding it. Reminisce about it but don't live in it . . . don't get stuck in it."

And finally, "Be occupied or focused on things and issues that are of interest and concern to you. Remain passionately involved in them."

Remaining passionately involved was one of Morrie Schwartz's gifts. His connectiveness, and desire to help and teach others along the way, are still in high gear.

During an interview he was asked whether he was afraid to die, and he responded by telling a story someone had just told him. He said there was once this happy little wave, rolling and skipping along the top of the ocean without a care in the world. Suddenly he looked ahead toward the shore and realized that he was going to hit it and crash to bits. He was headed right for it and there was nothing he could do. He was panic stricken.

Just then along came another little wave and asked him what was the matter. "Well," he said, "here I was happily swimming along, when I realized I'm headed for that shore— and I'm just a little wave who's going to crash and be broken into bits. That will be the end of me!"

The other wave then said something very wise and profound to the frightened wave. "Don't be afraid. You are not just one little wave. You see, you are part of a huge, never-ending ocean."

I suppose it's doubtful that you or I will ever meet Professor Morris Schwartz, but we wish him well on his journey. He still has much to give the world, despite the racing clock. By speaking out, this man will not only inspire his fellow sufferers, but make many others start thinking about how to make the most of their allotted time here. Even my 40 year old friend Dave, who has 32 years to go, may learn from it.

Thank you Professor Schwartz. I may never look at the waves breaking on the shore in the same way again.

Aren't we having fun?

A FRIEND and I were talking about something we had in common—both our mothers had spent the ends of their lives out of touch with reality.

We both knew the pain that came from watching them slip away from us. And it didn't matter whether the diagnosis was Alzheimer's Disease, Senile Dementia, or hardening of the arteries; as far as we were concerned, their conditions had the same ultimate effect—they became childlike and not at all like the people we had grown up to know fully and love deeply.

You would think this would have been a morbid conversation, but it turned out to be just the opposite. My friend John Fipphen, I discovered, had quite a different perspective on how to deal with a parent who becomes a child.

John's mother had been the wife of a physician and quite well known in her community. She was always involved in local affairs and lived a full, interesting and interested life as a wife, mother and later as a widow.

But, when she was in her late 70's she began to be forgetful and confused. John observed his mother's steady deterioration, and when her mind began conjuring up people and events that did not exist, he knew it was time for her to be placed in a home.

Many of us know what a traumatic event this can be. The walk down the steps of a nursing home after admitting a parent can be one of the longest in our lives. Even if the particular long-term care facility is known as the very best and most caring in the area, it is still a very long walk out the door that first time. It's not unlike the first day we leave our child at the new day care facility or kindergarten class. We are entrusting our most prized possession to someone else's care, and often, against their will.

Well, anyway, Mrs. Fipphen got all settled in at the home but continued on her path toward unreality, despite valiant endeavors of the staff to keep her in touch with the world around her. John made visit after visit with her, only to find that she didn't seem to know just who he was, or what it was that he was trying to tell her. Their conversations became more and more frustrating to them both.

Here is where John departed from the rest of us. He faced the fact that what his mother had become now was a child in adult's clothing, and he decided that if she thought as a child then why not spend their time together doing things that children like to do? Why keep trying to carry on two opposing levels of conversation, driving them both to distraction?

It wasn't long before good times began to reign in Mrs. Fipphen's room. Gales of laughter would spill down the corridor and the nurses would say, "Mr. Fipphen must be visiting his mother again." And sure enough, down in Mrs. Fipphen's room, John and his mother would be in the midst of a riotous spelling bee or similar childhood game, and they would be doubled up in laughter. John said that his mother would often turn to him and say, "Aren't we having fun?"

This twosome became famous in the home, and these spirited interludes continued on a regular basis until his mother passed away, a year or so later.

Now, all of us can't be like John, nor are all ailing octogenarians just like Mrs. Fipphen, but in their case, it worked. Afternoon visits between two young-at-heart people were laugh-filled interludes instead of tearful encounters.

It wasn't an easy decision for John. He knew there was a fine line between humoring his mother and being condescending and disrespectful to her. He did it with grace. He took the lemons life had dealt him and made fanciful lemonade out of them. And today he can look back on the end of his mother's life with a sense of satisfaction and with a smile on his face.

I asked him whether his mother ever had flashes of reality, or if any of her old spunky self ever surfaced during those visits, and he burst into laughter as he recalled just such a time.

One day he thought he would trick his mother by asking what the letters M-O-M spelled backward. He said she thought for a moment, then looked at him with a knowing gleam in her eye and said, "They spell WOW!"

Here's to the John Fipphens of this world who dare to swallow their pride and deal creatively and positively with seemingly impossible situations. And here's to those they humor, whose fancies are tickled sufficiently for them to look up at a comfortably familiar face and say, "Aren't we having fun? WOW!"

III. The Wee Creatures Among Us

"The sun and the moon, all creatures have an equal share in them."

—*Kazakh Proverb*

Living with a furry couch potato

YOU MAY not believe what I'm about to tell you. If I hadn't seen it with my own eyes I wouldn't believe it myself. You'll just have to either take my word for it or ask my cat Emily Dickinson; she'll back me up.

The event that changed my home life—possibly forever—began just before Christmas when my friend Carol mentioned a new video that was on the market—for cats. "Go on!" I protested. "You're pulling my leg!" But the next day she came into my office and presented me with my very own cassette entitled *Catnip Video*.

Now you have to understand that I am a latecomer to the VCR world. I bought one about a year ago, and except for the night I installed the thing and rented a couple of films to see whether it worked, I haven't used it since. So the day I brought home the cat video, I had all intentions of filing it away until the spirit moved me—like next year sometime. But after dinner I looked over at Emily the cat sleeping soundly on her favorite chair, and my curiosity began to get the better of me.

It wouldn't hurt to just turn the thing on, I thought, so I did. The video began with a brief written warning for all cat owners to make certain that the backs and sides of their TV sets were fastened securely, just in case their cats became so excited that they tried to crawl right inside the sets! (Emily was still comatose on the chair, so I knew this was the furthest thing from her mind. She was too smart for this kind of fool-ishness anyway!)

As the video ran, it soon became apparent it was a low-budget show as far as actors were concerned because the cast was made up entirely of—what else—real live birds and squirrels. As a matter of fact, the whole video consisted of close-ups of chirping, flitting, swooping, chattering birds and squirrels.

I was about to turn the thing off when I looked over at Emily and saw her ears suddenly beginning to swivel toward the TV, like two furry satellite dishes in search of signals. She was commencing to hear sounds which, up until now, emanated only from our back yard.

If I hadn't seen what happened next, I'd never have believed it. That cat actually opened her eyes and began to focus on the TV screen like a hunter on safari. She slipped slowly down from her chair and virtually slithered across the floor, hugging the edge of the room so as not to be seen—never taking her eyes off those blue jays and cardinals as they cavorted across that TV screen.

She then positioned herself behind a large planter just a few feet away from the TV, and peered long and hard through an opening in a cluster of philodendron leaves, stealthily stalking her prey and quivering from head to foot.

She waited until she felt none of the birds were looking her way and then made her next move—jumping up on the window seat and landing alongside the TV, where she proceeded to "hide" most of her body out of sight of those nuthatches and squirrels who were now in the video.

Now, you have to picture what was happening on the screen. The birds, at very close range, were flying into focus and landing on feeding perches just inches from my cat's nose. A few bird seeds would fall from the feeder and old Emily would reach her paw out quickly to try to catch them. And occasionally, although almost imperceptible to me, a squirrel would appear in the background, and Emily would pin her ears back and crouch down for the kill—just as if it were the real thing.

The most bizarre movement of the evening came when the birds suddenly took off in flight and headed toward the top corner of the TV screen with Emily in hot pursuit, leaping toward the back of the TV cabinet and trying valiantly to catch them.

She sat there that night as long as the video lasted. For about 25 minutes this cat, who never even noticed that we *owned* a TV before, sat there without so much as taking her eyes from the screen. She had found a new world. Emily Dickinson had entered the age of electronics.

Well, I'd like to say that this was an isolated incident and that Emily's TV watching was short-lived, but not so. In fact, just the opposite is true.

Gone are the evenings when I could sit by the fire and watch this beautiful feline sleep peacefully in her chair. In their place are nights when I'd prefer to have the TV turned off, only to look up and find Emily perched next to the blank screen giving me a look that says, "Where's my show?"

And that's not all. She has begun to watch "people" TV as well. Although *Wild Kingdom* and *Sesame Street* are high on her list of favorites, she also seems to like those vanishing squares on *Jeopardy!* and sometimes she takes special notice of Louis Ruckheiser and guests on *Wall Street Week in Review*.

My friend Carol, who got me into all this, reports that of her eight cats, five are now addicted to the tube. The minute they hear their show begin, they run into the room and line up in front of the set. (Except for Andrew, that is, who is a free thinker and prefers to sit up on top of the TV in hopes of nabbing some of these high-flying escaping birds.)

Besides that, Carol tells me that the other day she put on a relaxation video and looked up to find those darned cats lined up yawning and stretching in front of the set—and Andrew sound asleep on top of it—obviously all feeling the effects of the tape's soothing message.

There is no doubt in my mind that we have created a monster. My cat has become a couch potato and I'm beginning to feel a little guilty about it. After all, she came from a long line of felines who prided themselves on being shrewd and nonconforming, yet here I am "pulling the fur over her eyes" so to speak. She's been had.

Now you and I know there are no birds living in my TV set, but right now Emily thinks there are. I suppose some day she's going to discover the truth and be mad as anything at me. And I'm not so sure that this doesn't raise a philosophical question as to whether or not enticing a cat to watch TV borders on being inhumane.

Life will never be the same around here. I might as well go down to the video store and sign Emily Dickinson up for her own rental account. Just think of the possibilities: Alfred Hitchcock's *The Birds, One Flew Over the Cuckoo's Nest, To Kill a Mockingbird, Winged Victory, Night of the Condor, Birdman of Alcatraz.*...

Talk about wedding receptions!

THE BRIDE wore white. The groom wore navy. The worms wore pink. This was some wedding reception!

The happy couple had been married in Las Vegas a few months before, but since so few relatives and friends could attend, they scheduled a summer reception in the bride's hometown of Cape Porpoise, Maine. Not coincidentally, the annual reunion of her family—the Seaveys—was scheduled for the same weekend, so this assured a large turnout, not to mention food you could die for.

I left home that Saturday morning dazzled by the first sunlight we'd seen in days and drove toward what I thought would be a sunny reception by the shore. By the time I finally pulled in at the old Seavey homestead, however, the sky opened up and released a deluge. So much for sunshine on the wedding party.

The side lawn was graced by a large white elegant tent. It was complete with round-topped plastic windows, resembling french doors for letting the sunshine in. One glance at the sky told me they'd be lucky if any sunshine got inside that thing on this day.

I entered the homestead to take stock of what had happened to my friends the Seaveys since I last met with them two years before. Just inside the kitchen door I saw the Tupperware containers filled with Janet Seavey's sour cream pastries and loaves of Ruth McGinley's oatmeal bread, so at least their baking skills were still up to speed.

The young children of course, changed the most. The girls, who two years ago had shapes like uncooked spaghetti strands, now had developed breasts and hips and looked more like curly lasagna. The boys' voices had reached that unpredictable range where they went from soprano to baritone at scary intervals.

The adults' changes were subtler; there were more canes this year, and one walker. I noticed that the usual joking back and forth among the eldest seemed subdued, as if giving more stage room to their progeny. One thing everyone had in common was the excitement over the wedding reception.

After a bit of socializing, it was time for the festivities and we began filing into that magnificent tent. We soon learned that days of copious rain and a tent placed at the bottom of a hill did not make for an ideal combination—unless your name was Noah.

The first two or three steps under the big-top were cold and wet, but bearable. But as we ventured further we discovered just how *much* rain El Nino had brought us, as our feet began to sink down into the grass and soggy ground below. We asked where our table was, hoping for one right near the main entrance. No such luck. It was the furthest away, over in the opposite corner. With every step, our feet sank deeper and deeper into the lawn. Cold wet mud began oozing up over the soles of my sandals and then squishing between my toes. With each step came ominous sucking sounds as the earth drew on our feet like one giant Electrolux. I began to wonder whether I'd ever see my shoes again.

When I reached our table it was too late to save the shoes, and too cold to take them off, so I settled for putting my feet up on the rung of my metal chair and left them there.

Suddenly the Master of Ceremonies announced the bride and groom and we all (reluctantly) stood up to welcome them. They were in full bridal attire: the bride with her elegant white gown and he in his Navy full dress uniform.

As she entered the tent the bride, having been forewarned about the boggy dance floor, lifted her bridal skirts to her knees and we then saw that she was in her bare feet. Her groom had his dress shoes on, but was holding his pantlegs up as far as he could—probably figuring it would be cheaper for the Military to reissue him a pair of shoes than it would a new uniform. They smiled happily—but we all knew something they didn't—yet. Not only was the lawn soaking wet with mud oozing out of it, but along with all of that mud came the worms. Hundreds of worms. Zillions of worms. The place was crawling, slithering and wiggling with worms— big ones, all pink and shiny from having had days and days of beauty baths. This was a fisherman's paradise. We could have put a live bait sign out at the street and made some big money.

The lucky guests who lived nearby all went home and got their LL Bean waders and slogged around in those. The rest of us sat there with our feet up on the chair rungs trying to map out the shortest route out of the tent.

"All right, ladies and gentlemen," said the Master of Ceremonies, "it is time for the bride and groom to cut the cake—please rise." I could have killed him. The mud in my sandals had just begun to drain out—now here we go again. I never knew how many verses there were to that "The Bride Cuts the Cake" song.

Next came the dancing. I hoped the worms were ready for this. Seemingly oblivious to these little friends underfoot, a hardy group of line dancers got up and Macarena'd their hearts out—some with boots, some bare footed and some with shoes that would never see the light of day again. I began to worry about the worms. How many were being crushed to death under those dancing feet, anyway? Would they be smart enough to hide under tables? (Don't come to mine, please). Then it occurred to me that these things might actually be enjoying themselves. This may have been the most excitement they'd had in years. I was tempted to ask the disk jockey if he could play that old ditty, "Did you ever stop to think when the hearse goes by that some day you're going to die—the worms crawl in, the worms crawl out. . . ."

Mercifully for the worms, the dancers decided to move out onto the driveway (where there were fewer worms) and we took that opportunity to make our soggy exit. By then the sun had come out and many of us took off what was left of our shoes to dry our feet. Just as this process was about completed, however, someone shouted "The wedding cake and home made ice cream are ready. Help yourselves!"

"Where is it?" we asked. "Inside the tent, on the far side!" was the answer. A groan went up from the crowd.

The Seaveys won't forget this reunion for a long time and neither, I suspect, will the worms.

"... apparently dead—
hope it's not yours"

I CAME home the other day to find a note on my door from my neighbor. "Someone from the next street came around asking whether anyone over here is missing a grey tiger cat with white underneath. It was hit by a car in front of her house— apparently dead. Hope it's not yours."

I went to the back door immediately and gave Ralph Waldo my usual call. Ralph never came home in silence; he always meowed his way along from wherever he was when you called and kept it up all the way home, as much as to say, "I'm coming! I'm coming!"

But there was no "I'm coming!" to be heard this time. The only sounds emanating from the back yard were a few end-of-the-day chirps of some fortunate birds who had managed to escape Ralph's hunting forays. Otherwise, the silence was deafening—and ominous.

I went out to the garage and put a shovel and a box into the back seat of the car and drove around the corner to the neighbor's house. Sure enough, it was Ralph all right. I was relieved at least to see that this kind person had not only come looking for the owner, but had taken him from the road and laid him in a shallow box on her lawn, away from traffic. I went to her door and thanked her for doing so.

Next, I lifted Ralph into the car. He looked as if he'd just curled up in that box for a nap, the way cats like to do. His tiger stripes were as proud and shining as ever—no abrasions to be seen—but not a sign of life.

Deciding that I probably couldn't bury a cat in the yard of a condominium, my next thought was to get him to the veterinarians right away so that they could take care of burial. I rushed down to the office only to discover that they'd already closed for the day. Ralph would just have to remain in the car until morning.

I thought about how much Ralph hated that car—or any car. He was no fool. He knew that those odd cats who loved to ride were the exceptions to the rule. Just as real men didn't eat quiche, real cats weren't created to ride around in cars as far as he was concerned. This time, however, he had no choice. He would have one final silent ride to his veterinarians in the morning and I would say my goodbyes to a great little friend.

I'm getting used to life without Ralph Waldo now but there are still some reminders around—like the earrings.

On rainy days when Ralph was left indoors and I had the audacity to go and leave him alone, he took out his aggressions by scooping earrings out of my jewelry case onto the floor and playing cat hockey with them. Often I'd find them under a rug (after I'd stepped on them and broken them, of course) or more often under furniture or behind doors.

Ralph missed his calling—he could have been a high scorer on the Boston Bruins. I'm still in the process of retrieving the last of the earrings.

Ralph was a very vocal cat who didn't believe in suffering in silence. He never wanted to wait until I'd brushed my teeth in the morning before he was fed. He'd meow and pace the floor till I dropped everything and went out to the kitchen to open yet another can of his morning entree.

And if I went away for a weekend and left him in someone else's care I heard about it when I got home—for hours! I was scolded royally.

Ralph Waldo is the second furry friend I've lost to highway traffic in two years. Emily Dickinson met her demise right out at the end of our driveway one foggy evening, exactly two years ago this week.

All this, of course, brings up the issue of whether cats should ever be allowed to go outside. Recent reports indicate that the life span of outdoor cats is around three years. We all know exceptions to that, of course.

I have a friend who lives on a very busy street, yet her cat is outside day and night for most of the year, is deaf as a post, and is still going strong at 20+ years. Maybe cats like her get to use up the remainder of the nine lives which the less fortunate cats like Ralph Waldo (age two-plus) never live to utilize.

Then there is Tiny Tina Turner who lives with my sister in an eighth-floor apartment. I wouldn't be surprised if this feline outlives our whole family, given her lifestyle.

As far as I can determine, the closest she comes to exertion is when some bird happens to veer off course and swoop by the eighth-floor window, causing this frustrated tabby to crouch, salivate and ready herself for a conquest that will never be made. It's a pitiful sight.

Tiny Tina Turner didn't always live on the eighth floor. For a few years she lived on the third (top) floor in an apartment which had a small balcony. She became adept at climbing from that balcony up to the roof for some unique hunting expeditions. She would bring back down to the apartment everything from bats to bugs, proud as anything.

Now on the eighth floor, however, she considers it a good day if a spider makes its way up through the drainpipe into the tub so she can pursue it.

Whether cats spend their days inside or out is pretty much left up to us humans. If we want to have them for company, to be around for us to talk to when things get otherwise quiet and lonely, then we should keep them inside. But if we want a cat to live up to its potential as a hunter, then we should let it go out and take its chances, but keep the shovel and spare box somewhere in the garage, just in case.

I miss Ralph Waldo. From now on, who can I complain to when it's the night before a deadline and I can't get a column to come out right? Who'll finish the leftover milk in my cereal bowl every day? Who will patrol the back yard for encroaching mice and moles?

I am a cat person, so it's tempting to rush right out and get some other feline to take Ralph Waldo's place. But before I go and adopt some furry Robert Frost or Edna St. Vincent Millay, I think I'll wait a little while—at least until all my lost earrings are accounted for.

Allergy + sinus + mugwort = trouble

I SAT there in the allergist's office watching my arm to see what would develop. Sure enough, it didn't take long for a bump to start rising, and then another.

The skin test was doing its thing all right but the trouble was, I didn't know which pin pricks were which. Did that reaction mean that Ralph Waldo the cat would have to go or would I just have to hide indoors during the hay fever season?

All I knew for sure was that I was never bothered by allergies until two or three years ago. In fact, up until then I rather suspected that these maladies were fabricated by the drug companies in order to sell more nasal sprays. I wasn't too understanding toward my sneezing and blowing friends.

Once my own sinuses were causing me almost daily pain, it was a different story, however. I wanted to get to the bottom of it once and for all.

"Mold!" the nurse exclaimed. "You sure have a sensitivity to mold! Do you have much mold at home?" I began thinking she somehow must know about my habit of letting cheese go moldy in the back of the refrigerator.

"No," I lied. "I can't see whatever would be moldy at my house."

"Wait a minute" the nurse said, "what's this? Yes, here's another one. This one is for house dust." Mercifully, she didn't ask me if I had any of *that* at home—one lie per day would have been enough.

"There's another one—and I'm not too surprised—dust mites."

"Dust mites?" I asked.

"Here's a pamphlet—you can read all about them when you get home."

Next, I met with the doctor in the adjoining room. He looked over the nurse's findings and said a few "uh-huh's," the way doctors always do, and then repeated the list of things I'm allergic to.

"Dust, Hickory, Hormodendrum, Aspergillus, Pteronyssinus, and Mugwort."

Dust and Hickory I'd heard about, but the next three I could barely pronounce, never mind define. And as for Mugwort, I know it's in the Artemisia family but don't ask me what it looks like. Besides, I think it's an absolute crime that any growing thing has to be saddled with a name like that!

The doctor then proceeded to tell me how I could deal with these, my new enemies, and handed me more pamphlets which featured products guaranteed to help alleviate my aching sinuses.

"The good news is that I don't see why you'd need to bother with allergy shots," the doctor said. Those words confirmed my first impression of the man— he knew his stuff and wasn't going to complicate Hillary Rodham Clinton's health care woes by signing me up for treatment I didn't need.

I thanked him and went out the door clutching my pamphlets and trying not to scratch my arms, which by now were itching all over.

Later that night, in the privacy of my dusty and moldy house, I settled down to peruse the pamphlets. On the cover of one of them was a picture of a dust mite—the ugliest thing I'd ever seen. It looked like a black Idaho potato with six hairy legs growing out of it.

I got out my ruler and measured it—2 1/2 inches across! I prayed that this was not true to scale, but rather an enlargement.

According to the pamphlet, these critters live in rugs, overstuffed furniture, and mattresses. And (mercifully) they are only microscopic in size.

Here's the part that almost did me in. "On average, a bed contains two million mites. Each mite lives from two to four months, produces 20 droppings per day and each female lays 20 to 50 eggs every three weeks."

I didn't have the faintest idea how they knew this but I'd

have to take their word for it. I started to worry about whether my bed was sturdy enough to take all this. Two million mites times 20 droppings per day each can add up pretty fast.

Then I began to wonder whether mites have any kind of structured society—do they form colonies and hold elections? Is there a president mite and a first lady mite? Do they have schools for little mites? Is there much mite crime? Any need for police to be on dust mite duty?

Are there zoning laws so that certain types live in one section of the mattress while the others live in another?

Some of this information on dust mites may surprise you. Up until this moment you've probably been under the impression that only one or two of you were sleeping in your bed every night and now you find out that there could be two million more!

You still may be the only one(s) doing any actual sleeping in the bed because I doubt whether these dust mites get to shut their little eyes, what with all the babies they bear and droppings they drop in their short lifetimes.

The pamphlet (which by now I can barely stand to look at) went on to tell me how to get rid of these unwanted allergy producers.

First, you treat your carpets with a surefire mite killer for about $25 per rug. Once that's done, it says you may "vacuum the carcasses and excrement away . . ." Somehow it's difficult to think of things as small as dust mites having carcasses, but I suppose they do.

As for the bed itself, the solution is to cover the mattress, box spring and pillows with special plastic protectors. This is the first line of defense between you and your "roommates."

Besides covering my bedroom landscape with plastic, there will have to be some other changes made around the house. First, of course, I will have to become more intimate with the vacuum cleaner; it and I will be spending more time together from now on. Its cousin the dust mop will also be on a first name basis with me.

Next, there is my mother's handmade 9x12 braided rug in

the bedroom. If I am to wage a true war on these dust mites, this rug may have to go. Braided rugs, you see, have nooks and crannies, and while they may be all well and good for English muffins, they offer too much temptation for those little dust mites.

I used to wake in the night thinking of deadlines to meet and appointments to keep, but now I listen to see whether I can hear what any of my two million roommates are up to. So far, I haven't heard a single dropping or baby mite being born.

The disturbing thought just occurred to me that if I encase all these dust mites in those plastic coverings, will they die or will they just keep on birthing and dropping until the mattress explodes from the mass of carcasses and droppings that accumulate?

I'm beginning to wonder whether I might not have been better off just putting up with the sinus headaches.

This just might be a case where ignorance would have been a whole lot more blissful than having to spend the rest of my life going around listening for dust mites and watching out for an occasional patch of Mugwort!

Check-out time at the Mice Motel

THE ACTION is picking up at my house, and most of it takes place between my cat Willy Wordsworth and little furry cheese-eating things. You would think, seeing that a cat lives here, these rodents would consider moving to a neighbor's house because none of *them* have cats. However, I've canvassed them and not one admits to having mice.

I'm beginning to wonder just how effective old Willy is. Perhaps he's coming to the end of his warranty. In fact, he may be part of the problem. It's as if these mice are spreading the word among their friends that if they want to watch a cat go crazy, this is the place to come. If that's their intent, they are succeeding.

Day after day poor Willy sits atop the back of the wing chair in the living room, head cocked toward the ceiling, just listening to little scratchy sounds he hears clearly but which my human ears can barely detect.

Afraid that he would develop some irreversible neck muscle damage, I decided to go on the offensive and give him a go at those mice once and for all: I pronounced it open season on fast furry things. After all, if my state can declare hunting seasons for bows and arrows, rifles and the like, I could surely have one for hungry cats.

So one day, after letting Willy loose in the attic, I came back downstairs and waited for the action to ensue. Silence. I thought surely I'd hear the patter of big and little feet soon. More silence. After about an hour I decided to go back upstairs to see what was going on—what was Willy doing anyway? Well, what he was doing is what all cats do best—sitting and watching and waiting.

Did you ever notice how long cats can do this? They have powers of concentration second to none, especially if they think a mouse is at the end of their gaze.

106

Eventually, I began to hear movement. Some poor mouse must have made a run for it and Willy was in hot pursuit. Back and forth they went overhead. For a while it sounded like the Indianapolis Speedway and the laps were getting faster and faster. Momentary pangs of conscience surfaced as I thought of those innocent little mice being done in by what to them must look like a grey and white Tyrannosaurus Rex with whiskers. I know I could have used those Have-A-Heart traps, but then I would have to get in the car and drive them to some other part of town and let my little captives go, knowing all the while that every single one of them has an AAA map route right to my door.

When the commotion died down I let Willy back in the house. "Well," I said, "what happened up there anyway?" Now here is the maddening thing about cats: they never tell you anything. They're silent about their conquests and don't drive around town in their pickups, displaying their latest kill on the hood the way other hunters do.

It wasn't until the next time I went up in the attic that I got my answer. Willy certainly saw action up there—and so did my fiberglass insulation. It was tossed and turned all over the area instead of on the floor where it does the most good. Evidently, in order to chase these mice from their hiding places, Willy must have ploughed right along under the batts of fiberglass in hot pursuit of a mouseburger. I don't imagine this was too good for Willy's health, but at least I know he saw combat of some kind.

I thought perhaps that attic foray would end my problem—but no.

A few nights later I was sitting on my sofa minding my own business, and Willy was doing likewise on his chair, when he suddenly sat up and twirled his radar ears toward the dining room. He obviously heard something. I went out to investigate and saw nothing and returned to the sofa. Cats don't put much store in our surveillance techniques, however, so in a flash he was off the chair and in the dining room. Sounds of a scuffle ensued and in a few seconds Willy strode into the living room with a mouse hanging out of his mouth.

Now when a cat comes toward you with a live mouse in its mouth it's a good news-bad news situation. The good news is that he cut down the mouse intruder population by one. The bad news is that he is either going to eat it right there in front of you and make you sick to your stomach or worse yet—let the thing go and drive you both crazy. Willy opted for the latter. The mouse, of course, scooted under my sofa—to live another minute or hour or perhaps even days. I would rather sit through ten reruns of *The Lion King* than watch one cat tormenting a mouse before the kill—especially if he has any idea of doing it in my bedroom in the middle of the night.

This in mind, I beat a hasty retreat to my room and went to bed—but not before I shut the door and stuffed pillows under the opening at the bottom of same to ensure no mouse could get through. Then, since the door latch isn't always reliable, I pushed my treadmill up against it—just for good measure—and a good night's sleep.

In the morning I realized how absurd my treadmill barricade idea was. After all, I'm bigger than a mouse. Besides, even Willy knows that nowhere in history has it been recorded that a puny mouse has eaten a human being alive.

The next night I learned that the previous evening's cat and mouse game had either been fruitless or this little fellow had a cousin. About two o'clock in the morning I was awakened to find Willy on my bed, running and pouncing from one end to the other. I soon discovered that he wasn't running by himself, a little furry thing was just ahead of him. Now I don't know much about mice, but I do know they are small enough to get under bed covers and that was enough for me. This time I sought safety outside of my bedroom, barricading Willy and his friend inside. This time I stuffed the pillows on the outside of the door.

At this writing I don't know where the mouse is, or mice are. I wouldn't mind giving these mice a winter home if they just wouldn't scurry around so fast, scaring me out of my wits. If mice would just learn to *walk* instead of scamper, I'd be willing to negotiate. If they'd saunter across my floors, I'd let them live inside until spring. Of course, whether Willy will agree to such an arrangement is another story.

Dealing with a broken relationship

ENDING a relationship is no way to wind up one year and start the next, but that's what's happened. I should have known it wouldn't work anyway, since we didn't have much in common. Moving in together was probably a bad idea from the start, since I've been on my own for so long.

As anyone who has lived alone for any length of time can attest, you develop some peculiar habits when there's no one around to observe you on a daily basis. Set mealtimes, for instance, are almost nonexistent. With just your own schedule and appetite to cater to, you tend to eat when the spirit moves you, and dinner time is not exactly a scene from a Martha Stewart TV special. Eating occasional meals straight out of the refrigerator containers, for instance, is a far cry from the way most of us were raised, but it happens sometimes.

Another live-alone habit I had to consider when the relationship took hold was talking to myself. Although I know some married folks who do this, the people who really have the art perfected are those of us who live alone. In my case, I'd try to hide it under the guise of talking to my cat, Willie Wordsworth, but even he knew better.

Anyway, I never thought much about all of this until the ill-fated house sharing venture began. I want you to know right up front that moving in together wasn't my idea. It happened rather serendipitously and almost overnight. Even though each of us had to give up a certain amount of freedom (and bad eating habits), I have to admit that it was nice living with a partner who didn't meow and shed fur all over the house.

Actually, we got along quite well. In fact, the only time there seemed to be a space problem was in the mornings when we both wanted to use the bathroom sink at the same time. Morning after morning without fail, the very moment I would decide to brush my teeth, my partner would appear at the same place.

We finally worked out a compromise. While I used the sink and rattled off my plans for the day (it was so good to have someone to tell them to), the new light of my life would climb up and down on the bathroom mirror.

As you can imagine, it wasn't easy getting a foothold on such a slippery surface and sometimes it would necessitate either starting all over again, or taking flight from the mirror altogether; ladybugs have a tendency to do that.

(Oh—I guess I didn't mention that my new friend was not of the human kind. Sorry. Details sometimes elude me.)

No, this tiny creature was a friend in miniature—a cheery thing providing a delightful spot of color to my day and asking very little of me in return. It had come in from the cold during the Fall hunkering-down period that these beauties go through. But instead of sleeping through winter, it decided to keep me company instead.

I only saw my housemate in the mornings at the mirror and never at any other time, but it fascinated me. Despite its feminine name, I wondered about such things as, for instance, was this a male or female ladybug? Harkening back to my freshman biology class I decided there had to be one of each sex in order to make them so prolific, but if that's so, why do they call them LADYbugs? Unanswered questions aside, I became very fond of this little friend.

Then one morning it happened. The inevitable, I suppose. I was at our favorite meeting place as usual when I noticed there was no ladybug friend on or near the mirror. Terror overcame me as I imagined that perhaps Willie Wordsworth had suddenly pounced on it as a tasty breakfast morsel. Then, to my relief, I saw that it had only changed perches—it was down in the sink itself. I made a mental note to turn on the water just slightly, so as not to disturb my little friend, then I got ready for work.

The next part is almost too gruesome to tell. Just before leaving the house, I rushed back into the bathroom to brush my teeth. Without thinking, I turned on the faucet full blast. I looked down just in time to see the little red-and-black-spotted body swirl once around the sink and then disappear down the drain.

So that is my tale of the broken relationship—a tragic ending to a pleasant interlude, really. As I said at the outset, I probably should have known it wouldn't last, since we had so little in common—but the ending was still sad, just the same.

Well, soon it will be a new year and I know there will be other relationships, and perhaps even other ladybugs. As a matter of fact I am certain of the latter because just yesterday while taking down curtains in my guest room, I discovered not one, but a large cluster of red-and-black-spotted round beauties sleeping away the winter atop my window frame.

They should sleep well there until spring, but then again, you never know. I think I'll keep the mirror shined and ready, just in case.

IV. The Family in Folly and Elegance

"We owe a cornfield respect, not
because of itself, but because it is food
for mankind. In the same way, we owe
our respect to a collectivity, of whatever
kind—country, family or any other—not
for itself, but because it is food for a
certain number of human souls."
—Simone Weil, *The Need for Roots*

While waiting for Hope

THE LAST time my daughter and son-in-law increased their family I was at the hospital for all 25 hours of labor. This time, I will be on duty a lot longer because they've chosen a different route—to China.

Somewhere in an orphanage in the city of Shao Guan is a little seven-month-old baby girl about to be adopted into our family. Found abandoned at the train station, she is one of thousands of unwanted female babies in China who, if it were not for adoption, would have a bleak future at best. This is one of the reasons her new parents have decided to name her Hope.

During the two weeks they are in China, my mission will be taking care of my grandson Andrew. A piece of cake, right? How difficult can that be? After all, it's only been 30 years since I had a four-year-old of my own. We shall see.

DAY 1. Andrew's mother and father leave for the airport at 4:30 a.m. for a 25-hour flight. *My* assignment for the day pales by comparison; I only have to find Andrew's nursery school.

I immediately designate him as co-pilot for the next two weeks, and we start out. At the first intersection I say, "Right, left, or straight ahead?"

"Straight ahead" comes the little assured voice from the car seat in the rear. This goes on for a couple of intersections, when I finally begin to sense we are nowhere near the nursery school.

At the next intersection, I happen to observe the body language of the co-pilot in my rear view mirror. he is saying "Straight ahead," pointing to the right! These two weeks may not be as easy as I thought.

DAY 2. Well, so much for all my worrying that I'd forget to pack my alarm clock. When you have a four year old in the house, you don't *need* an alarm clock. He *is* the alarm clock. Unfortunately, he's set according to the sun because he bounds into my room at 5:45 a.m. and doesn't run down until after the sun quits for the day. Perhaps the next time his folks go to China they'll go in December when the days are shorter.

DAY 3. We go to McDonald's for breakfast. Not because *he* wants to go but because already I have a need to see people who are taller than my belt buckle. Grandparent types give me knowing glances as I sit at my table sipping coffee from one of those cups with the "Caution—Very Hot!" warnings on them, and watch Andrew's breakfast get cold. He has been swallowed up in the big plastic play yard and I worry about whether I'll ever see him again.

DAY 4. Sunday. Andrew locks the cat in the bathroom and there is no key on the outside. We go to church to pray for a solution. There is.

DAY 5. A phone call from China. Today they take a three-hour train to the orphanage. They are so pleased to find that by Chinese standards this is a small one with only 30 baby girls to place, sleeping three to a crib. Andrew assures his parents that Hope's crib at home is all ready, complete with teddy bear.

DAY 6. I'm getting into the swing of the nursery school routine. It makes me feel young again as I interface with the mothers of the Yuppie and X generations. Today I bound out of the car and sprint to the building to pick up Andrew when some little kid opens the door, takes a look at me and shouts "Hey! Somebody's grandmother's here!" You can't win them all.

DAY 7. My daughter is a wonderful mother—she thinks of everything. On the refrigerator is a calendar she made with lift-up tabs. Under each day's tab she tells how many days before they come back and shows a number for Andrew to match on a wrapped daily gift up in her closet. (Remind me to speak to her about today's gift, a 950-piece set of Legos. Assembly is definitely required—by me!)

DAY 8. I get a reprieve from assembling Legos. Five-year-old Steven from across the street comes over to play. He is a whirlwind—an accident waiting to happen—but a lovable one.

He endears himself to me when before dinner (to which he invited himself) he thanks God for the "wunnerful, wunnerful supper" and his "wunnerful friend Andrew and his wunnerful grandma." This boy definitely has a future in politics.

DAY 9. Another call from China. The adoption papers are complete—Baby Hope is now with them in their hotel room, beautiful but with a fever of 102 degrees and crying constantly. I decide that this is not the time to tell them that Andrew threw up all over the kitchen floor today, or that I spent three hours in the local hospital emergency room with a case of gout (yes, gout). We'll save these details until they get back.

DAY 10. Andrew and I drive to the local library and look at a big globe to see how far away China is. I show him all the water between here and there and hope this explains once and for all why his parents simply cannot take a bus back home.

DAY 11. Today Andrew informs me that he intends to marry his friend Samantha when he grow up because "I wuv her very much!" "Besides," he adds, "if we get married, then we can *dance* togever." I see that my daughter has handed down the same detailed sex education tips her mother did.

DAY 12. It's swimming lesson day at Gold's Gym. The place is filled with people who don't look as if they *need* a gym. There isn't a love handle in sight. After the lessons, I take Andrew to the women's locker rooms to shower. Sylph-like naked bodies of all ages parade by as Andrew and his intended bride, Samantha, shower together. I'm suddenly acutely aware of my own body, and thankful I can keep my clothes on.

DAY 13. I present Andrew with a "genuine" Indian arrowhead, and launch into an educational session on Native Americans. I told him how they probably lived right there where his town is, and of how resourceful they were.

Just as I was feeling pretty good about my presentation he asked the question. "Nana-Jo, what ever happened to them Indians anyway?" I mumbled something about their having made reservations, and hoped he'd think they went out for a long dinner. No sense telling him the ugly details of their fate. When he's older I'll tell him how glad I am that they eventually got some revenge on us pale faces by taking our money at gambling casinos.

DAY 14. We're coming into the home stretch. Tomorrow's the big day. Andrew has done a remarkable job taking care of me. He is a delightful little guy—and I say that as a proud grandmother.

At bedtime, after his three stories (two with the light on and one in the dark by flashlight), he starts singing a song he's learned this week from a video entitled "Alexander's Terrible, Horrible, No-Good Day." In the story, Alexander, who is momentarily tired of having older brothers, sings it. Ironically, it's called "If I Could Be An Only Child." Andrew croons himself to sleep singing that song, unaware that he has just concluded his very last day of being an only child himself.

DAY 15. It's 10 p.m. and we are at Gate 41 at Logan Airport waiting for Flight 36 from San Francisco. The first of the new parents steps off the plane carrying a Chinese baby— she looks exhausted but happy. Then another. Finally Andrew yells "There's my dad!" And right behind him is my daughter with a little soft snuggly carrying case around her neck and inside is a little dark-haired baby girl with sparkling eyes.

Andrew rushes from me to them, and the long wait is finally over. But as I get closer and see that beautiful face of this tiny, bewildered, little girl named Hope, I know instantly that this is no ending. This is just the beginning.

Letter to a Chinese grandmother

PLEASE allow me to introduce myself. First of all, I too am a grandmother, with all the rights and privileges that come with such a title. I get to be amazed, delighted, and sometimes worried over my children's children. I love to see them coming and hope they feel the same about me. I am expected to carry photos in my wallet, always at the ready in case some unsuspecting person comes along and casually asks about my grandchildren.

I am writing this letter because you and I have something very special in common. But perhaps I should start at the beginning—or at least the beginning as I know it.

Last year my daughter and her husband flew to your country with a tiny photograph tucked into their suitcase. It was the picture of a baby girl, only a few months old. Though the photo was of poor quality, when it arrived at their house you would have thought it was a Rembrandt, because it gave them the first glimpse of what their new daughter would look like.

First, of course, they shared it with four-year-old Andrew, who was to become this little one's big brother. Then, in what seemed like only minutes, they had made copies of the picture, faxed and e-mailed versions to friends and relatives, displayed it prominently on the refrigerator, (which is what we do in America to things of which we are most proud), and they called everyone they knew to say it had finally arrived.

This little photo was the first tangible sign that their long struggle with first infertility drugs, and then adoption procedures, would soon be over. Even before their bags were packed they knew what they would call this little girl—her first name would be Hope, because her new life would symbolize hope for her, and for them as well.

The trip to China went as planned and soon a beautiful six-month-old girl, with the same face as the one in the photo, was placed in my daughter's arms. It was time then to leave the orphanage and begin a new chapter in the life of their family.

A year and a half has gone by now. A lot has happened in that time. Little Hope's development was restored to the level it should be, her fitful sleep pattern began to subside, she learned to sit up, walk, stand and now run with no problems, and her shiny black hair has grown almost long enough for a ponytail. In other words, she is a healthy and happy little two-year-old.

By now you are probably wondering just what this has to do with you and why I am writing this letter. The answer is simple. You see, you and I really do have something very special in common; we are both grandmothers of this sweet little girl named Hope.

For me, of course, it is wonderful to be the visiting grandmother. I reap all the benefits of having a little girl run over and climb into my lap—or hear her learn how to say my name—or talk to her on the phone.

I am the grandmother who can buy her the little bracelet with colored jewels that light up when she touches them. I am the one who tells people how smart she is. "Could dress herself way before she was two," I boast. "Has been going to a Montessori school since she was 18 months old!" As if I had anything whatsoever to do with the innate intelligence this precocious little one possesses.

This is why I am writing to you. You see, lately the closer I bond with this child, the more I am consumed by the thought that you are somewhere in that vast country, completely left out of this process.

Do you wonder about this little child with the almond-shaped eyes and stick-straight shiny black hair? Do you grieve at not knowing her, or her not knowing you? I want you to know that I, the other grandmother, am haunted by this.

Surely, all families who engage in adoption, international or not, must experience this to varying degrees. I know my daughter and her husband do. While thankful beyond words that they have such a little girl, they often try to put themselves in the place of the parents who had to abandon her in the train station that November day.

At their home last summer they hosted a gathering of adopted Chinese girls who came to America when Hope did. Before they ended their time together they held a brief ceremony in remembrance of those who had to give these children up.

They all went out into the yard and released red helium balloons in tribute to, and in memory of, these biological parents. The children, too young to understand, thought it was fun to see the balloons rise in the air. The adoptive parents, however, took it as a serious symbolic act of compassion.

Those of us who live in other countries will never understand the practice in China of forcing families to give up little girls—and sometimes boys. We can only wonder whether one ever gets used to it.

In the meantime, thoughts of you seem to possess me; I feel I need to reassure you somehow that Hope is now in a wonderful family, with a chance for a very bright future. Her adoptive mother and father are dedicated parents who know how to balance love with discipline and adoration with sensibility.

Her brother alternately loves and tolerates her—just as most big brothers do. And Sarah the cat, aware of Hope's swiftness of foot, still prefers to worship her from a safe distance.

As for Hope herself, you would be so proud to see how well she is doing. She is a happy, well-adjusted two-year-old. She is curious about everything that moves and breathes. She never walks unless there's no room to run. Climbing across the top of jungle gyms never fazes her, and one of her favorite foods is Chinese noodles.

She also has a mind of her own. Don't even think of having her put on her blue shoes if she fancies the red ones that day. She loves to laugh, and when she does, her entire face crinkles up into a mass of exploding character lines.

Perhaps she will grow up to be a teacher, for when it is

time to sing songs she sometimes makes it quite clear that "just the girls sing now" (the "girls" being my daughter and myself). Later on, she will declare it time for "just the boys" so Andrew and his dad can join in.

Or perhaps she'll be a singer. One night my daughter called me on the phone so I could listen to Hope, who was upstairs crooning herself to sleep with the Happy Birthday song. There from her snug bed, with the beautiful framed Chinese print hanging on the wall above her, over the electronic monitor came this little voice: "Happy birthday to you…" Only by then she had evidently exhausted every name she knew, so before she finally drifted off to sleep we heard "Happy Birthday dear SOMEBODY, happy birthday to you!"

It will soon be a new year for us — and a few weeks later, you will be celebrating the beginning of your Year of the Tiger. Though many of our customs differ, one common belief we share is that it is the time to start over. Time to clear out the old and begin anew. That is what I am attempting to do with this letter.

Though you may never see it, perhaps some other grandparent who is estranged from a grandchild will—and they will know that in the days and years ahead, those of us who now make up the new family unit will not forget them or stop grieving for them.

For the new year I wish you inner peace, a grandchild or two to sing to, and hope for brighter tomorrows.

Ellen and the sea slugs

WHEN MY niece invited me to her wedding I accepted readily, but deep down I dreaded it.

Not that I didn't want to see her get married, but the thought of sitting through another wedding reception didn't thrill me. The older I get, the more I pray that my car will break down somewhere between the wedding and the reception hall.

I'm speaking of those traditional, formal receptions where you are assigned seats with people you either don't know at all, or *do* know and would just as soon *not*. Then you and those table mates vegetate for an hour and a half waiting for the bride and groom to have their photos taken by a waterfall somewhere.

Add this to a backdrop of ear piercing music played by a disc jockey who's brought a van load of CDS which he plays on one speed—LOUD—and you've got the kind of reception which for some of us spells pure torture.

This niece of mine, however, is what a friend of mine refers to as "a piece of work"—a musician who's big on fun and short on details—so this wedding just might be different. I gave her a call the week before the big day to see how things were going.

"I finally got the band signed up for the reception," said she. "Ellen and the Sea Slugs from Maine," she exclaimed. "They're a contra dance group and you pay by the slug. I'm having six slugs!"

Six slugs, I thought to myself. Suddenly my dread of a humdrum reception faded and I looked forward to the big day.

As I suspected, the wedding turned out to be like the bride—warm, delightful and innovative. This was verified when they rolled the bridal carpet down the church aisle. It had hand-drawn colored pictures all over it—sketches of favorite places and things of the bride and groom. This set the tone for the day.

When I arrived at the reception, the Slugs were already earning their money: one accordionist, one guitarist, one pianist, one violinist (from a Peruvian symphony orchestra), one bass fiddle player and one young man playing the bones (that's like playing the spoons). Six Slugs, all present and accounted for and sounding very good and lively.

It turned out that Ellen herself couldn't make it so the young man on bones was designated Head Slug and lead dancer. It was up to him to get the guests out on the floor for some fancy footwork.

I surveyed the crowd for recruits and decided that this guy had his work cut out for him as far as volunteers were concerned—at least with our side of the family anyway. Right away Aunt Alice stated that she hadn't danced since the '50's and that was just fine with her. Uncle Fred held on to the video camera for dear life, glad he had been given so vital a function that he couldn't possibly take time out to contra dance.

To add to the dilemma, many of the wedding guests had volunteered to bring the food, so half the women were out in the kitchen, elbow-deep in Tupperware containers of potato salad and hummus, preparing the meal.

So here was this poor Head Slug trying to get a respectable number of folks up on the dance floor in order to teach them a few steps. Suddenly, he came over to me—either in desperation or because I was close by—and asked me to be his partner and to help teach the dances.

This was refreshing, I thought to myself, since so often when I go to weddings alone there's no one to dance with because single men in my age bracket are on the endangered species list. I accepted the invitation and soon I was whirling around the floor in waltz time with this agile Head Slug who was probably 20 years my junior.

He was very light on his feet and, I think, a bit surprised to find that I could actually dance. Then when the music stopped he whispered to me, "You're good! I hope you'll help me teach a tango later!" At that point after executing more revolutions around the floor than I had in 25 years, I was thankful just to get back to my table and rest, never mind the Tango.

When it was time for the Tango, however, the Head Slug was back, so we got into the drama of the Latin beat—dipping and sliding and all. At one point as I careened across the floor I caught a glimpse of my daughter snapping pictures of me, catching on film for posterity the one and only time she'd ever seen her mother doing the Tango—and with a slug at that!

The final dance was a waltz interspersed with slow Russian folk dance steps. We were very graceful, if I do say myself, covering every inch of the dance floor. For a moment there, as I whirled around the room with this young good looking Head Slug from Maine, my dress became a size 8 once more and those annoying marshmallow-like upper arms felt taut and youthful. I was 17 again, spinning around at the Saturday Night dance with a boy named Maurice, the best dancer in our High School.

When the dance ended, the Head Slug looked straight at me and said, "You know, I really enjoy dancing with young women." For one swift, wild millisecond I thought he meant me, but then he added, "but I find *they* can't dance—only you *older* women know how to dance."

As I headed home that night, crushed by the sudden comedown of my brief but glorious moment in ballroom history, I tried to tell myself all wasn't lost. The bride looked radiant, the decorations on the aisle carpet were delightful, and last but not least I thought, how many other women in this world will ever be able to say that they danced with a Head Slug?

I smiled all the way home.

Waiting for my sister
to get married

I HAD to sleep in a crib until I was ten years old. I know psychiatrists could probably have a field day telling me how this has led to my idiosynchracies, or at the very least how it accounts for my tendency to sleep curled in a fetal position. But you would too if you made your nightly home in a space that small for the first 3,650 nights of your life.

I still can remember that crib. It was made of wrought iron and painted white. It had high bars on four sides, but of course by the time I escaped from the thing, the fourth side had been in the 'down' position for ages.

In case you are wondering why on earth I had to sleep in a crib for so many years, the answer is simple. It was because of my oldest sister. Our family didn't have the money to provide amenities like private bedrooms and separate beds for all of us, so Sister #1 and Sister #2 had to share a double bed. The understanding was, that once the elder sister married and moved away, I, Sister #3, would graduate to the double bed with my other sister—a dubious promotion, but at least a step up from the iron prison I was used to.

Since Sister #1 was 14 years my senior, it would stand to reason that I might be liberated from the crib at least by the time I was 5 or 6 because people married young in those days. Prospects really looked good since she began dating a boy during high school, and they got serious right away.

At some point I remember he got his pilot's license, and on Saturday mornings he would fly over the house in a little two seater plane and tip his wings. I viewed this as such a true gesture of love and passion that marriage certainly couldn't be far behind—or so I thought!

While the courtship continued and the years went by, I

waited while I watched my body outgrow the crib. My feet began to stretch out through the iron bars, and turning over became a monumental maneuver.

To make matters worse, the room the crib was in was a small, low ceilinged afterthought in the mind of whoever built that house. Its walls were white wood siding and it had one small window, one small sewing machine, one small sewing basket, one small crib and me, one not-so-small person trying desperately to get out! In the summertime, hornets nested between the partitions, and I could hear them on hot August days. In winter the room was cold, being furthest from the one central heat register.

I would have given anything to ask her when she intended to get this marriage show on the road, but in those days older sisters commanded respect, so I had to settle for small clues to give some semblance of hope. She began to have her hair done every Saturday morning—surely a sign of something.

Then one evening, a silverware salesman came to the house and spent hours interesting her in buying flatware for her hope chest. I discovered, alas, that the filling of hope chests could be rather misleading. Girls could have them stocked crammed full of goodies for literally years before anyone came along and asked them to marry them. Still, I looked to any sign of domesticity on my sister's part as a definite chance for my freedom.

As years went by I reluctantly began to put up touches of my own in "the little room." First, tiny snapshots of cats and dogs, and then friends, and finally, full color magazine photos of John Payne and Clark Gable. The room, although according to my parents "just temporary," was beginning to appear to be my permanent home.

Finally, however, the happy pair ran off and got married and it was a glorious day for all. He gained a wife, she gained a husband, and I gained half a full-sized bed!

Now I was faced with another slight problem—Sister #2. I had to learn how to live with a high school cheerleader who was going through the typical rebellious stage. But half a loaf—or bed in this case—was far better than none.

I found you can learn all sorts of things when you share a room with a sister eight years your senior. I mastered the art of walking in her high heels, and I learned there were more kinds of underwear than the plain cotton type from Montgomery Ward. I discovered that females can get very moody around a certain time of the month. As a matter of fact, my mother owed a debt of gratitude to her because by the time she got around to offering me any information about "women things," Sister #2 had already taught me by osmosis. So there were pluses as well as minuses that came with my half of a big bed.

My second sister had more mercy on me than the first did, for she left home after only two years of our living together. So finally, at the ripe old age of 12, I not only got to have my own room, but my full size (and well worn) bed; my seemingly never-ending quest for my own space ended.

Someone asked me recently how I remember some of these details from my youth. I responded that I actually have a very poor memory, but some things, like being ten years old and having your legs stick out of the foot of a crib, are not easy to forget.

Once in a while, it comes back to me in a dream—but I never mind as long as I'm assured of waking up in the morning knowing that I won't have to wait for my sister to get married again. Once was enough!

Signed and sealed,
but better hold the delivery

THE OTHER day I got a call from my sister in Florida telling me that she and her friend Charlotte had decided to be cremated—not together, of course, but when each of their times comes.

It seems they were down in the community building in their mobile home park and heard a man from some cremation outfit give a pitch for an all-inclusive $500 special. Sort of a final one-size-fits-all deal.

"It's part of a chain," she explained.

"You mean like McDonald's or Wal*Mart?" (I restrained myself from suggesting that there could be a cremation chain called *Ashes R Us*).

"You know what I mean," she said, "and you can be shipped from just about anywhere—even Canada."

Now as far as I knew, Canada wasn't high on either my sister's or Charlotte's list of places to visit. They're more apt to head for Las Vegas or New York. But if having Canada thrown into the deal made them happy, so be it.

"Just think about it," she continued, "here I am in Florida and the family cemetery lot is way up in New Hampshire. Rather than going through the expense of being carted all the way up there in some casket, it makes better sense to me to consolidate and ship, so to speak."

I told her it made sense to me too, and that she and Charlotte ought to be commended for their decision. I then reminded her that our other sister made that same decision years ago. I remembered the day she called, all excited because she'd been to our cemetery to inquire about the price of lots and found out that if she got cremated she'd save money. "For $40 I can be put in with mother and dad!" she exclaimed.

Which all goes to prove, I suppose, that when it comes to matters like burial arrangements, we Snow sisters are either very foresighted or very cheap—or both.

My sister's children weren't too happy to hear that their mother signed on the dotted cremation line. I suppose that was to be expected. They are afraid that she knows something they don't know and that she must suspect she's about to slip on that final banana peel of life.

"You just tell them, " I said, "that you and Charlotte are still out there playing bingo, going to shows, engaging in cut-throat card games, and driving back and forth to New England at the drop of a hat. Tell them you're still planning to go to New York for Christmas, Las Vegas in the spring, and who knows *where* in between. That might reassure them."

Well, the cremation phone call lasted a long time, but I figured that since it was her nickel and since she was going to save on those shipping charges some day, she could probably afford it. I hoped that by the time we hung up she felt somewhat relieved that I agreed that she'd done the right thing. But just in case, I sent her a little something in the mail the next day.

It was a one of those blank greeting cards with a black and white photo of two 1940's women on the cover. There they sat out on the lawn on a pair of folding metal chairs, Queen Elizabeth type hats on their heads, pearls adorning their earlobes and necks, pointy horn-rimmed glasses perched on their noses, white toeless shoes laced onto their feet, and their purses clutched firmly in their laps. They were obviously smiling at something in the distance.

On the inside I wrote this message: *Congratulations to you and Charlotte for signing up for cremation. Look at it this way—at least you're still able to make decisions!*

So I say, good for them—they are all signed and sealed—but let's hope the "delivery" part doesn't come for a long time!

Knowing nuthin' about birthin' no babies

WELL, LADIES, it has finally happened. Medical research has determined that we women who were once thought to be beyond child bearing age, can now have babies! Women in their 50's, 60's, and even older can, if you'll pardon the pun, conceivably give birth by utilizing eggs from women much younger than themselves.

That sure shoots holes in the old joke that claimed the reason women our age didn't have babies is that we'd forget where we put them, doesn't it?

Medical science may have opened quite a Pandora's box. Just explore with me for a moment the possibilities here—good and bad.

Let's say I decided to have myself a baby when I reached 65. For starters, I would probably be eligible for senior discounts on my maternity clothes, Medicare might pick up the doctor visits, and my friends could throw me a rousing surprise baby shower down at the local Social Security Office. So things wouldn't be all bad—besides, how noticeable could stretch marks be when your flesh is getting to be a mass of wrinkles anyway?

If all went according to plan, I would have my baby in the summertime, when TV reruns are on, so there'd be no chance of missing anything new. I suppose my due-date would be the day after I retired from work, just so I wouldn't get a taste of what it's like to sleep late in the morning. And as far as those nightly feedings are concerned, heck—at my age I'd be up two or three times a night going to the bathroom anyway, so a few more waking moments wouldn't bother me.

Now let's suppose this baby turns out to be a boy, and when he's eight years old he wants to join the Cub Scouts.

That means that at the ripe old age of 73 I will be plodding down to den meetings in my orthopedic shoes, helping with camping trips by knitting ear warmers and mittens, and whittling little Pinewood Derby race cars with swollen, arthritic hands. Admittedly a challenge, but with a little extra Geritol each morning, I could probably hang in there.

And just think how helpful I could be with his school homework. I didn't spend all those years watching *Jeopardy* and *Wheel of Fortune* for nothing!

I know, you are wondering what I'd do when this child became 18 years old and announced that he wanted to go to Harvard. No problem! At age 83 I would just get my fellow nursing home residents to put on a few more food sales and bingo games and we'd wipe out that tuition bill in no time.

This is not to diminish the importance of this new medical finding, however, because for childless women who had thought it too late for them, this is good news. The biological clock which they'd feared had run out, may have just been changing over to Fertility Savings time.

My own two children and their spouses have been looking forward to being parents for some time, but so far there are no baby announcements forthcoming. Extensive tests have been done and assurances made that there are no medical reasons to preclude their becoming parents at some time in the future. Although there are definite feelings of disappointment and worry, there has also been a great deal of joshing about whose fault the delay really is.

It has even been suggested that since this problem involves both my children, it's just possible that when I gave them my famous "birds and bees" lecture years ago, I left out some vital bit of information.

Well, I want you to know I have done my part toward solving this dilemma. Not only have I gotten out my knitting needles, I have passed on to my son and son-in-law an invaluable tip I read in Dear Abby. It stated that men wishing to become daddies should store their undershorts in the freezer. Now I ask you—what more can I do? The rest is up to them.

In the meantime, however, there is always this new never-too-late motherhood discovery. Who knows? Maybe years from now when my daughter and daughter-in-law are in their 60's and I am in my 90's, "baby lightening" will strike all three of us at the same time!

This late-in-life baby stuff is scary business. Science just may have gone too far this time. I liked it the way Mother nature planned it in the first place—a span of years to have babies, then the rest of our years to recuperate!

Take my mother-in-law . . . please

WHAT DO you call your mother-in-law? Mom? Mrs. _? Hey You? By her first name?

If your answer is "by her first name," you are in the growing majority, because it seems that it is becoming harder and harder for us to refer to someone else's mother as "Mom" or "Mother." It just doesn't roll off the tongue easily, so we opt for "Mary" or "Alice" or some other first name instead.

Interested in the subject for years, I once took an informal in-law poll among my fellow workers at the office and received some interesting responses.

The first woman I spoke with said her husband, after 16 years of marriage, would still rather die than telephone his in-laws' house because when one of them answered, he would have to ask for the other one by name! And he had no name for them, other than Mr. and Mrs. Sanders.

This reminded me of a wonderful letter to Ann Landers from a woman who said she was being driven absolutely crazy by her son-in-law. Every time he came to visit he followed her around the house like a shadow—he was never more than an arm's length away.

Finally she confronted him one day and asked just why it was that he seemed to be following her so closely. He answered, "Because I never know what to call you, and I figure if I stay close enough, I won't have to call you anything!"

My poll found several people in that category.

One young woman told me how delighted she and her husband were that her in-laws had moved to their state, and were much closer to them. I said it was indeed a compliment to them that she liked having them so close.

"Oh, that's not it!" she exclaimed, "It's just that now they live near enough so when they come to visit they don't have to stay overnight with us, and we're not stuck with them for weeks at a time."

Poor in-laws! They sometimes have to take a bum rap in life, especially mothers-in-law. Since time began, they have been the butt of jokes. Standup comics could always count on a laugh whenever they alluded to the mother of the woman they married.

For years we had to listen to the old standby about the comedian's mother-in-law who rushes out with the trash one morning—hair in curlers, old tattered robe on—and she calls to the trash truck driver, "Am I too late for the garbage?" and the burly driver shouts back, "Heck no, lady. Jump right in!" Luckily, those jokes are fading from the scene, but not fast enough.

One day while conducting my poll in the corporate wash room, I asked a total stranger at the other sink whether she had a mother-in-law.

She replied, "Well, I did have one, but she passed away last year," and as I prepared to offer condolences she added, ". . . and not a moment too soon!" Evidently the quality of mercy is still strained, as far as mother/daughter-in-law relationships are concerned.

You may not believe this, but I know of a family where the daughter-in-law got so sick and tired of her mother-in-law popping in unannounced to see the grandchildren, she came up with a rather unique but drastic solution.

The next time her mother-in-law came to visit she found the door locked, and tacked to it, one of those store-front signs that say "CLOSED." Beneath that there was a clock set at a time when the house would be "OPEN" again to the mother-in-law. Speaking from a mother-in-law's perspective, I find this harsh treatment.

The "meddling" image makes it difficult for those of us who are parents-in-law to know how to act these days. We bend over backward to be as impartial and unobtrusive as possible, but it's not easy. Lord knows, I've tried to help the cause.

I never put any emphasis on gourmet cooking or spotless cleaning in our house while the children were growing up just so I wouldn't set any superwoman precedent for my son's bride or daughter's husband to have to live up to years later. My children would never have reason to say, "My mother did it a better way," because chances are, I didn't.

Getting back to the name situation: I found that many couples have solved the what-to-call-the-inlaw problem by simply waiting until the first grandchild comes along. Then they just adopt whatever name the youngster happens to call the grandparents. Some of the names are bizarre, but they serve as a godsend to many a shy son-in-law.

My son-in-law calls me Joann, and so far, that sounds just fine to me. Of course, some day in the future I wouldn't mind if he decided to change it to something else.

"Grandma" would have a nice ring to it.

My father was in overalls— and sometimes hot water

MY FATHER was in overalls. I don't mean he wore overalls but his business was making overalls, or jeans as we call them today. He learned the trade back in the days when overalls were strictly utilitarian and the idea of them becoming high fashion someday was inconceivable.

My grandfather owned an overall factory in northern New Hampshire and my father started out there as a helper, then worked his way up to be a cutter. Although I never found out why, he and his father had a falling out and my father moved to another city to work for a competitor, eventually becoming the plant manager.

It was this overall business that, for a short time at least, caused my mother to have a bout with jealousy. You have to realize that these were the days before my mother got into the workforce herself, when she had time to let her imagination run rampant as far as my father's male magnetism was concerned.

I suppose if you were to walk through the old overall plant as I often did you might see how this could happen. As far as the eye could see were rows of women—tall ones, short ones, skinny ones, and plump ones—but all women.

These were the pieceworkers, angled over their whirring sewing machines and stitching against the clock in order to make as much money as they could in a single day. The machine noise in the place could be deafening, but even over that din you could hear the stitchers carrying on fragmented conversations laced with laughs and bawdy jokes.

Only two men worked in the shop. The cutter was always a man because of the physical demands of the job. He would pile foot-high layers of denim on the cutting bench, then with

137

his tailor's chalk draw out the patterns on the very top one. With a vertical electric blade, he'd slice through those layers creating dark blue pantlegs, pockets and waistbands to produce a never-ending stream of pieces in order to keep up with the women and their machines.

The other male was my father, the manager. This meant that on any given day the woman-to-man ratio in the shop was perhaps 40-2. It was this ratio that must have bothered my mother. It wasn't so much that she distrusted my father, but all those stitching hussies—well that was another story.

Sensing my mother's jealousy theory, I decided to do a little investigating of my own. Since I often walked to my father's shop after school to wait for a ride home, I decided that I might as well make a study of these femme fatales who, according to my mother, were such a big attraction for my father.

One day, just after closing time, I sat in the family car observing the women as they filed down the wooden staircase and onto the pavement toward home. Many still wore their aprons, some were old enough to be my father's mother, and all of them looked as if the only thing they had on their weary minds was getting home to their families.

I decided then and there that my mother could quit her worrying. Not a one of them looked like a major threat as far as I could see. These were just decent hard-working women working their fingers to the bone trying to make some kind of a living.

So much for my mother's suspicions.

There was, however, one other flareup of the green eye of jealousy in our house. And that all started because of the chickens.

My father, besides being into overalls, decided to go into chickens for a while. He soon learned that having a yard full of chickens meant too many eggs for one family; even though there were six of us, we could only eat so many omelets a week.

It made perfect sense then for my father to find himself some customers and establish a weekly egg route, and this he did. Every Thursday evening after supper he would set out on the route, delivering his boxes of peewee, medium, and large eggs.

Although never a chicken fancier herself, my mother managed to co-exist with the brood, including the part where they had to be rounded up and killed for our Sunday dinners—pinfeather plucking and all! She didn't even mind the egg route because my father seemed to enjoy it so much.

The problem was that he got to like his night out every week so much that after the last of our chickens had gone to that Big Chicken House In The Sky, father continued to go out on Thursday nights. He never said where, he was just going "out."

This never did set well with my mother and those twinges of jealousy made an appearance at our house again. I suppose her imagination ran wild, thinking that my father was holding trysts with Joan Crawford or Hedy Lamarr, or maybe one of those sewing machine ladies from the shop.

My sister and I were talking about this period one day and she told me that on many Thursday nights she would go to the movie theater and who would she see in the third row, all by himself and snoring through the film, but father. I hope she shared this with my mother at the time.

Fortunately, my father was one of the easiest going souls you could meet. Gregarious and generous to a fault, everyone loved him (even those women at the overall shop) because he was a nice guy.

I tend to think he was always faithful to my mother, despite her concerns. How bad can a man who makes overalls, raises chickens, and sleeps through movies be, anyway?

Fathers are just memories in my house now. I had my father for just 22 years and my children had theirs for only half that amount of time, making Father's Days bittersweet. I try to avoid the advertisements about what to give dad on Father's Day; you can't give a barbecue grill to a memory.

Yet I still love to observe the fathers of today. I watch my son taking such an active role in his sons' lives and I am encouraged about the future of fatherhood. Some of this may come from new age enlightenment, but I like to think that some of the best of it came from genes handed down from fathers before him—overalls, chickens, and all.

Letters to my mother

HOW SAD that when we die we aren't given a one day grace period in order to come back to take care of any unfinished business here on earth. A second chance to say the things we wish we'd said along the way—or to apologize for some things we did say. It doesn't seem too much to ask does it, to have just 24 hours to wind up all those matters filed under "unresolved"?

For instance, I would give anything to have such a day with my mother. It's not that we had any lingering animosity between us; on the contrary, as the baby of the family I had the luxury of doing some extra bonding with my mother once my older siblings married and moved out. Being born so far behind the others, I was often referred to as an "afterthought" or a "mistake" but somehow those names never bothered me—until, that is, the day I found the letters. It's because of those letters I would like to have my mother back, if only for one day.

I was just sixteen and getting ready for school one morning when I came across them in the bottom drawer of my mother's dresser. She had left for work earlier, but since we often exchanged things that came under the category of "accessories" I knew she wouldn't mind my borrowing a scarf.

My hand suddenly came upon a small stack of papers in the rear left corner of the drawer. Curiosity got the better of me and I lifted them out and discovered they were letters. The word "dearest" jumped off a page at me and I somehow knew this letter was not from my father; it just didn't sound like him. This correspondence had to be from one of my mother's suitors in her pre-marriage days.

But as my eye skimmed down the page, I read a sentence fragment I've never forgotten: "...you and Joann and I can go away..." it said. I looked at the date at the top of the page and saw it was not written before my mother married, but just a few weeks after my birth.

The letters suddenly felt like ice in my hands and I never read another word, except for the signature. I recognized the name as a man well known in our community as a church musician. He had been my mother's voice teacher.

Hands shaking, I put the papers back in the drawer, rushed to the bathroom to be sick to my stomach and then ran out the door to meet my friends for our walk to school. It was one of the longest days of my life.

As the months went by I found myself staring at my father, looking for resemblances between us. After a while I came to the unscientific conclusion that he was indeed my real father, but some lingering doubts always remained.

Years passed and yet not a word of the letters was ever discussed by my mother or myself. Then one day when I was home from college, and at an age when I knew everything and my parents could tell me nothing, a rare argument arose between us and I blurted out "his" name. My mother stopped short at what she had been doing, stared at me in disbelief, and then resumed her activities as if nothing had ever happened.

I never spoke his name again, although there were many opportunities to do so. After my father's death, my mother and I spent a great deal of time together yet there never seemed a good moment to broach the subject of this man and what their relationship was.

Finally, in the last years of her life, my mother's memory began to fade and confusion was setting up houseroom in her mind. I distinctly remember one afternoon, when she and I were on a long drive, I suddenly realized that this might be my last chance to ask her. But somehow each time I began, I found myself changing the subject. The words just never came.

At one point I spoke with my mother's sister about the letters. She was not surprised by them, but *was* surprised that I'd known about them all those years.

She told me I didn't have anything to worry about as far as this matter was concerned, but she did say that my mother and this man had a strong attraction for each other. "They were well matched," she said, "and they had music in common."

It wasn't until after her death that I spoke with my aunt about the letters. She was not surprised by them but was very surprised that I'd known about them all those years.

Straight away she assured me that all their meetings took place in her living room, and involved music lessons. But then she did admit the strong attraction each had for the other. "They were well matched" she said, "but they were both married, and in those days, divorce was out of the question." What she didn't say was something I already knew; my parents' marriage was not made in heaven. It was not a bad one, and they made good parents for the four of us, but I always felt they were misfits in many ways, and I sometimes wondered whether my mother's life would have been a happier one, had she been able to marry the other man. I would never know the answer of course, but now at least I'd found some of the missing puzzle pieces.

The story didn't end there.

Just a few years ago I learned from one of my sisters— almost inadvertently—that in a state of depression shortly after my birth, my mother tried to end both our lives. Fortunately, someone came home unexpectedly early that day and found the gas jets turned on full and my mother sitting in front of the oven with me in her arms.

You see now why I need this one extra day with my mother. At long last I would like to open this subject that was hidden away for so long. I'd tell her how frightened I was when I found those letters—and apologize for intruding on her privacy. I'd assure her I never expected her to tell me the details, but wished she could have shared some of that heavy burden with me or other family members during her lifetime.

On this one day together we could look at the situation in the sunlight of two adults. We would cry and maybe laugh over it and then go out to the kitchen and have coffee and big helpings of her tasty apple pie topped with slices of sharp cheddar cheese. Just like the old days. Then after the last crumbs of her Crisco and lard pie crust were gone I would ask one final thing. I would ask that she forgive me for writing and publishing this story.

Knowing my mother, I think she would understand that this was written as a reminder to those who still have their mothers to take care of unfinished business now. Whether it's telling them they love them, discussing family histories or resolving personal differences, they should not put it off.

Finally, I would tell my mother that on the one hand I wish I'd never opened the bureau drawer that morning, yet on the other hand—and perhaps only she would understand this—I'm so very thankful that I did.

Mothers and sons

THE SPAN of time between a little boy's first day at school and when he turns 30 or 40 or even 50 can be amazingly short as far as his mother is concerned.

No matter what our sons have accomplished since they outgrew peanut butter sandwiches and lunch boxes, we mothers tend to freeze them in time so that they are always our little boys. It may not be productive and it may not be right, but many of us have a difficult time admitting that those intervening growing-up years that turned boy into man ever existed.

It isn't the same with daughters. We mothers don't suddenly wake up one day and find that our little girls have reached adulthood without our knowing about it. That's because we've spent years identifying with them through every agonizing puberty problem, broken romance, and miscarriage along the way. In a sense we grow with our daughters and through them, so we're much more in tune with their evolution.

But since we've never been boys, we don't do this with sons. Perhaps that's why we never let them grow up—at least not in our minds and hearts.

The mother-son relationship is a fascinating one. I especially like to observe families where the only female in a household is the mother. She is more apt to be placed on a pedestal and adored in that all-male setting than in a home where a daughter has broken through the mother's mystique on a female-to-female basis. Even if their role is that of sole disciplinarian, women who raise only sons enjoy a special seat of honor in the family circle.

It's no secret either that mothers are often easier on their sons than they are on their daughters, expecting less from them and praising them more.

My own daughter once pointed out this fact to me when I would insist during her teenage years that she make the grand sacrifice of carrying her supper dishes from the kitchen table to the sink—a distance of about three feet—while I didn't seem to make those demands on her brother. Instead, I would clear his dishes from the table myself, without even thinking about it. I was guilty as charged.

Sometimes, sons can do no wrong in a mother's eyes. When I worked in the nursing home field, I observed first hand the way the patients would look forward to a son coming to visit—and talk about it long after he'd gone—even though this male offspring might only come twice a year and stay for 10 minutes.

There were some outstanding exceptions to this rule, of course, like my neighbor Arthur who would not only visit his 98 year old mother daily, but stay the whole afternoon talking about baseball and a million other interests they had in common. Yet when all was said and done, there was no question that he was still her little boy. "Why didn't you bring me the tan stockings I asked you for yesterday—in the top drawer, Arthur? You got these in the second drawer and they are grey!"

Arthur, in his 70s, was back in rompers again.

The daughters, on the other hand, could come to the nursing home every week and make sure mom had nice new clothes, or take her out for a ride, yet they often got taken for granted. It's almost expected of the daughters somehow.

My daughter and I are quite close—the older we become, we share more and more in common. We talk on the phone often, just as I did with my mother. Sometimes there are thoughtful calls like the one the other night.

The phone rang and she said "I thought you might like to hear Andrew singing himself to sleep—I've got the baby monitor turned up high so you can hear him." Then sure enough from a two-year-old's cozy crib in a darkened bedroom, right through my phone receiver, came the recognizable strains of "The Eency Weency Spiiiiider" and we both laughed. Sharing can come easily between mothers and daughters.

My son and I talk on the phone too, but once he's finished bringing me up to date on my three-year-old twin grandsons, the conversation begins to grind to a halt.

I tell myself it's because he is the least talkative in the family, but I suspect it's also due to something else. Despite the fact that he is a husband, father of two, homeowner and successful in his job, I still picture him playing with Matchbox cars and earning badges in the Cub Scouts. It's a bad habit we mothers have trouble breaking.

Sometimes I don't know what triggers the subjects of my columns, but there's no doubt this time. As the recent madness of a California dream gone wrong unfolded on your television screen and mine, and O.J. Simpson finally gave himself over to the L.A. police, I couldn't help notice the one last thing he did before climbing into the cruiser and heading for jail.

He called his mother.

Though you and I may never know the substance of that conversation, we can probably be sure of one thing. As far as Mrs. Simpson was concerned, that was no sports hero or TV celebrity she was talking to. Neither was it the father of her grandchildren, nor even a grown man who had just been the object of a police hunt watched by millions.

When his lawyer, doctors, and the police all prepared to take O.J. Simpson the man to jail, he was on the phone with someone who saw him quite differently.

As the world watched and waited, Mrs. Simpson was talking with her little boy.

Christmastime and Ironing Boards

I AM finding it more and more difficult to keep up with some of the holiday traditions. For instance, I have finally succumbed to having an artificial Christmas tree. It wasn't an easy decision. In fact, on the day I bought the thing I considered assembling it at the store, tying it onto the roof of the car and then driving around town awhile just so people would think it was real!

Another tradition I see falling by the wayside is the one which had me out in the kitchen for hours making my Spumoni cakes, Swedish rosettes and painted cookies. I now go to a church that sponsors a cookie walk each year, where I buy the most gorgeous assortment of decorated cookies you've ever seen. Then when I serve them I conveniently forget to mention that they didn't come from my own ovens.

We do have one tradition in our family that has lasted a long time, and it only happens once in every 25 years or so. It has to do with Christmastime and ironing boards. You might think the two have nothing in common, but in our family they do.

It all started years ago when four of us fledgling career women were sharing a fourth floor walkup on Commonwealth Avenue in Boston. Our stately brick home looked out upon the treelined street leading down to the Boston Gardens and the Common.

Once you climbed past our first three floors, however, the elegance began to fade. Unless you call "elegant" rooms spartanly furnished with offerings from the Goodwill store and a kitchen with only a hotplate for cooking. The apartment wasn't a palace, but it provided a comfortable backdrop for our lives as we did balancing acts between city life and all its temptations on one hand, and our first post college jobs on the other.

These were wonderful years which seemed as if they'd go on forever. But one day the inevitable happened. One of our group decided to move out and get married.

After she left, it didn't take us long to discover that among the things she had contributed to our cozy nest was an ironing board—and of course, what she gaveth, she also tooketh away. This was in the days when clothes dryers were considered luxury items, so irons and ironing boards came under the category of "vital equipment."

Realizing the urgency of the matter, one of the other roommates said she would purchase a brand new replacement. The only problem was that in no time at all she too up and married and took that ironing board with her. So it became a tradition in the house that whoever owned the ironing board would be the next to get married.

Enter Dick Duncanson.

We had been discussing marriage for some time but hadn't made any definite commitments. He was finishing divinity school and I was sure that the job I held as a greeting card editor was going to catapult me right into a flourishing career in journalism. So marriage seemed out of the question, or at least it did until that one particular night.

It was a snowy evening just two days before Christmas. The doorbell rang and as I went to answer it I looked over the banister to see suitor Dick starting up that first flight lugging what appeared to be Christmas gifts.

It wasn't until he got to the final flight that I saw what he was carrying. He had a small jeweler's box in one hand and in the other he was carrying—an ironing board! "Well," he said, "we have a tradition to uphold here, don't we?"

Many Christmases have gone by since then and with the exception of telling our children of the old ironing board story, the tradition became nothing more than a pleasant memory—until, that is, one Christmas season not long ago.

The phone rang one evening and it was my son calling to announce his engagement. He had just presented a diamond ring to his girl friend, then as I started to congratulate him, his new fiancee got on the phone and exclaimed, "It happened in the most interesting way. The doorbell rang and I looked over the banister to see him climbing the stairs and guess what he was carrying? He had a small jeweler's box in one hand and in the other he had . . ." I knew even before she finished that an old tradition had been reborn.

Today I have three grandsons. They are still quite young, but sometimes I can't help wondering whether in 25 years or so the world will still have such things as ironing boards. For the sake of holiday tradition—and true love—I surely hope so.

A vacation with sun,
surf and—no TV?

WE'D JUST walked into the little place which was to be our seaside summer vacation home for the week when Joey, half of the set of seven year-old twins, looked around and said, "Hey, there's no TV! Where's the TV?"

His father was ready with a snappy answer. "That's because this is a cottage."

"What's a cottage?" came the next question.

"A small house," said his dad.

Then I, as matriarch on this trip, felt it my grandmotherly duty to elucidate: "Remember the Three Bears ? They lived in a cottage. So did the Seven Dwarfs."

"And they had no TV?"

"No TV!"

By now, RJ, the other half of the twins, had inspected the small rudimentary kitchen.

"Hey—there's no microwave here! Did the Seven Dwarfs . . . ?"

I explained that dwarfs didn't have microwaves either.

We were in for quite a week of withdrawal here. No TV, no Nintendo, no favorite videos. How would these kids ever adjust? We decided the sun had better shine or we'd be up against it.

I unpacked my things while the small fry emptied their back packs of what appeared to be 500 Beanie Babies. At least, I thought, it was a step up from those menacing looking action figures of last year.

Now it was time to decide who sleeps where. Let's see. Two bedrooms with a double bed in each—that just didn't match up with two boys, one dad and one grandmother. I surveyed the well worn couch in the living room area, wondering how my body could keep from rolling off it during the night. Suddenly Joey said, "Wow! What a cool couch! Can I sleep on it—PLEASE?"

He'll never know how this question brightened the outlook on my vacation. I was able to have my own bed in my own room—and he was king of the couch, only falling off it one time.

The next morning RJ got up at 5:50, wide awake and talking a blue streak. So at 6:00 the two of us headed out—hands filled with slices of bread to feed the seagulls. It was rather nice, actually. Although this boy spends much of his time concentrating on trains and trolleys, he transferred his attention to gulls, crabs and clams quite readily, even though none of them had wheels.

When we packed the sea-gull bread it never occurred to us what else inhabit beaches at that hour of the morning— dogs! Though banished for most of the day, between 6 and 8 in the morning the sand definitely belongs to dogs and their accompanying people. One thing those mutts had in common was what they were there for. Now their masters claim it's so they can run on the beach, but upon careful observation it became clear their main activity was looking for a place to relieve themselves. Their caretakers, if responsible citizens, brought along two very important items: a scooper of some kind and a plastic bag.

"Are those people cleaning the beach?" observed RJ.

"In a way," I replied, feeling a twinge of pity for the dog walkers whose mutts relieved themselves in the first two minutes of their walk, meaning that their masters spent the rest of the time carrying around the evidence.

Just then one of the canines discovered we had bread in our possession. As soon as we'd throw it out to the birds he would come tearing at us, lunging for bread. We finally distanced ourselves and several gulls were served take-out breakfast, compliments of a boy and his grandmother.

We then turned our attention to another early morning beach phenomenon, the man with the metal detector, sweeping back and forth over the sandy shore in search of his fortune. He proudly brandished a large solid gold ring he had found, and proceeded to tell us of 60 others he had unearthed in the past year.

This evidently registered deeply with little RJ, and days later he asked just how that man was able to find all those people so he could give their rings back. I muttered something about finders-keepers and hoped this wouldn't undo all the things his parents had taught him about not pocketing things which weren't rightfully his.

At vacation's end, two tired but happy boys and a dad headed off for their Pennsylvania home in a car filled with memories, once-occupied seashells and New Hampshire beach sand. It was then I made a horrible discovery: they had left "Sly," a favorite Beanie Baby, behind. I pictured their father having to listen to wails of dismay for the next eight hours and knew there was only one thing a respectable grandmother could do. I threw the plush little fox into the car, revved up the engine and headed out after them. As I started up the highway a sleek black sports car raced by me going at least 80 mph. Okay, I said to myself, if he can go that fast, I can too because this is an emergency. I increased my speed, 60-65-70-75 . . . then it hit me. How would it look in the police report, anyway? *Grandmother on Beanie Baby mission arrested for speeding.*

I decided to quit while I was ahead. I turned around and headed for home. After all, I'd had a marvelous vacation enjoying the little cottage, my family and the sun and surf. And beyond all that, the telephone didn't ring once!

That's right—the Three Bears didn't have phones, either.

Memorial Days then—and now

I CAN still see Colonel William Duncanson, my father-in-law, on the week before Memorial Day, climbing over the terrain of the local cemeteries, arms laden with little American Flags to decorate the graves of veterans. He did it every year, no matter what the weather; no matter how he felt. Right up to the year he died he did it, willingly.

This grave decorating didn't come without a price, however. Each year, almost without fail, some irate townsperson would phone him to tell him in no uncertain terms that he had the nerve to skip so-and-so's grave. He never claimed to be infallible, but he also never bothered to tell the caller about the constant battle he had with vandalism and flag stealing. Each year after he did his decorating, he would have to make a follow-up trip just to replace those flags which had already been stolen.

But these weren't the only flags he put up. There was always one more—a much bigger version. A patriotic man, nothing would do each year than for him to shinny up two tall trees on either side of his driveway to suspend between them what my children always considered to be the biggest flag in the nation, moth holes and all.

Then on Memorial Day itself, the Colonel would be Grand Marshall of the Parade. Still as thin as he was in his World War II days and dressed in uniform, he'd proudly lead his sometimes rag-tag group of marchers from cemetery to cemetery. If a marching band of any size happened to show up, it always made his day.

Our family had a ringside seat since the Duncanson house was on the parade route between cemeteries. This was the home my mother-in-law and her children grew up in. A comfortable structure with a wrap-around porch and a large yard dotted with a cluster of gnarled old apple trees, well climbed by generations of small Duncansons.

People would start to gather with their lawn chairs around 10 o'clock, and by 11 we would hear guns go off down at the lower cemetery, signaling that they'd soon be coming up the hill.

When the marchers finally filed by, usually hot and tired from the climb, they'd have long forgotten which foot they should be on, the High School band windpower was diminished to the point where the drums were the sole accompaniment, and there were holes in the formations indicating where weary dropouts once were. To our children and others along the route, however, you would have thought it was sponsored by Macy's. We would watch until the very last Cub Scout, Brownie and Campfire Girl had trailed out of sight, then we'd say what a great job the Colonel did again.

Finally, to the sound of the old flag flapping in the breeze over the driveway, we would gather at the side of the house to cut boughs of Grandma's lilacs to take to the cemetery in the afternoon. This was a family day like no other.

What ever happened to Memorial Day, anyway?

Is it just in our family that the meaning and observance have disappeared? Is it because the Colonel and men like him aren't here to string flags over driveways any more? Has it gone the way of all Monday holidays—an excuse for a three day weekend and nothing more?

If blame can be placed anywhere, perhaps it can be directed at the accelerated times in which we live. Turning off our TVs and computers long enough to concentrate on those we've loved and lost—war or no war—has become almost impossible to do. It doesn't fit in with our schedules.

Sadly, it isn't just the parades, flags and marching bands we have abandoned—it's the pausing to remember. That's what we have lost. And sadder still is the fact that somehow we know we may never get it back again.

Of apple trees and anguish

THE APPLE growers' signs were up all over the place this fall telling us not only to come and pick our own, but to bring the whole family for a day of fun. Well I'm sorry, but somehow or other I never looked upon picking apples as fun.

When I was five years old we moved to the country where, among other things, we had a row of apple trees stretching along one side of the property.

At first, my father was quite attentive to these trees, spraying and pruning just as the books said he should. After a while, however, his enthusiasm began to wane and the apples took on just two functions in life—to become fair game for itinerant worms and to fall on the ground so as to necessitate clearing away.

That's where the family came in. Every fall, we either picked healthy apples or raked up rotten ones. While admittedly I wouldn't have missed climbing those apple trees as a youngster for anything in the world, the process of picking apples was not much fun for those of us who had to do it.

When I was in my teens, my friends and I looked upon apple picking merely as a way to make money. We would answer advertisements from the big orchards in the next town and spend the days either picking (when they trusted us on the ladders) or sorting out the bad apples from the good as they came tumbling down into a large trough. We always ended our day with either sore muscles or scraped knuckles or both. If you had suggested to us then that apple picking would one day be regarded as family entertainment, we probably would have laughed you right out of the orchard.

I am sure one reason for my present attitude toward apple picking stems from a day that comes back to haunt me every year at this time. Though it wasn't my original intent to air it here, I find somehow I can't do otherwise.

We were thirteen years old, and my friend Pat and I were on our way home from a neighboring town where we spent the morning and early afternoon picking apples at a large orchard. Coming home was always the best part of the day because not only was the work ended, but we got to ride on the back of the big flatbed truck with our hair blowing straight out in the wind and our feet dangling over the sides.

Since my house was just over the town line, I was the first to be let off that particular day, and as I jumped down from the truck, Pat called, "Why don't you come down to my house for a while?" I said something to the effect that I probably should go home. "Oh come on! No one's home at your house now anyway!" I was looking up the long driveway toward my empty house, trying to decide, when the farmer driving the truck yelled "Hey kid, make up your mind, we haven't got all day! Are you getting back on the truck or not?"

My house up there on the hill suddenly appeared very lonely to me, and I decided to climb back on the truck and spend the rest of the day with my friend. She lived down in the city, four miles away, and I always enjoyed escaping to civilization whenever I could.

When we got to Pat's house, I called my mother at her job to tell her where I was, and I remember that we spent the rest of the afternoon relaxing after our hard day at the orchard by playing Frank Sinatra records and talking about boys, which was regular fare for girls our age.

It was later, during supper, that the phone rang. It was my mother. "I have some sad news for you—your uncle Charlie died today..." I can still remember the shock of those words. When you are thirteen years old, death notices don't come close to home too often. I recall I couldn't comprehend how someone as young and healthy as Uncle Charlie could die so suddenly. And of my three uncles, he was the one who was closest to my brother and sisters and myself.

It wasn't until I got home that night that I learned the rest of the story from my mother. "Uncle Charlie didn't just die—he took his own life here in our garage while we were all away."

I guess I don't have to tell you how the phrase "while we were all away" affected me. Guilt came pouring over me like volcanic lava. I could have been home. My apple picking workday was over by mid-afternoon. I was heading for home by 3 p.m. I was the one who stood at the bottom of that driveway making up her mind about whether to go home or to get back on that truck. I was the one who decided in favor of Frank Sinatra tunes and girl talk about boys. I was filled to the brim with remorse.

The day after the funeral, I was sitting in a classroom at the junior high school when a boy named Chuck suddenly stood up and shouted across the whole room, "Hey guess what I found out! Old Man Hurley killed himself—right in Joann's garage!" I remember that I jumped up from my seat and screamed back at him, tears streaming down my face, "No he didn't! No he didn't!"

But of course he did, except Chuck never knew the half of it. He didn't know about the part where I stood at the bottom of the driveway deciding whether or not to go home that day. He didn't know about me getting back on the truck.

The road not taken that day has haunted me ever since. I might have arrived in time to thwart my uncle's plan. I might have been able to find him before the carbon monoxide had exacted its toll. Even at my age, I surely would have known enough to open the doors or turn off the ignition or call the police or something that would have saved his life. In my mind, I've been able to rewind that film and replay that scene many times, and it's always the same: I'm waving goodbye to Pat as the truck drives off toward town without me, and I start up the long driveway.

What would have happened next is anyone's guess. I might have arrived at just the right time, yet on the other hand, an intervention by me might not have been the best thing for Uncle Charlie. He was a very thoughtful and deliberate man and like so many others before and after him, he must have decided after all that this world and he could no longer coexist.

Many apple picking seasons have come and gone since that day, and the orchards are once again alive with sounds of laughter and excitement. Whole families are filling those bushel baskets with Macs and Cortlands in anticipation of home made apple pies.

But this idyllic New England scene notwithstanding, I am sure you will understand when I say that as inviting as an autumn day in those orchards might be, I can never go there again. I still miss Uncle Charlie

Reflections on a loved mother

THERE is something very perpetual about mothers. They often seem to be with us, even when they are miles or years away. In fact, it is not at all unusual for us to encounter glimpses of our mothers even long after they have gone from this earth.

We hear ourselves saying the exact things to our children as they did to us, complete with the same voice inflections. We use facial expressions and exhibit body movements that are unmistakenly inherited from them. And no matter how old we become, whenever we find ourselves in situations that call for a little "I told you so" advice, they seem to be standing there looking over our shoulder, prodding us on.

And when we come upon these things unexpectedly, it is both unsettling and comforting, all at the same time.

One day, I was walking past a store window when I looked up suddenly and saw the reflection of my mother staring back at me. My mother had been gone for more than ten years, so seeing her there was startling at first. Then, in what seemed an eternity but in fact was no more than an instant, she was gone, and I realized that the face I saw was my own.

In that brief moment, my emotions carried me on a roller coaster ride from yesterday to today—finally coming to a stop by a warm feeling that comes only from revisiting the most cherished people of our lives.

I went home that day to try to capture in verse what that brief encounter meant to me, and what similar events might mean to countless others who have experienced that same magical ever presence of the person known as Mother.

MOTHERS REFLECTED

I had a sudden vision
Of my mother the other day —
I was rushing past a row of stores
When she came — and went away.

It was bittersweet to see her
In the window of that shop —
The reflection was so fleeting
That I almost didn't stop.

Years had passed since I had seen her,
And yet here without disguise
Were those unmistaken frown lines
And those large and haunting eyes.

And I almost said, "How are you?"
And, "How wonderful you're here!"
But before I had a chance to speak,
She began to disappear.

And the window glass got cloudy —
But I'd just time to define
That I had become my mother —
And that face I'd seen, was mine.

So I walked away the wiser,
And I couldn't help but smile,
For I thought I'd lost my mother
Yet she'd been here all the while.

Joann Snow Duncanson, a graduate of the University of New Hampshire, began her writing career as a humorous verse writer for Rust Craft Greeting Cards in Boston. After a period of years spent raising her family, she renewed her interest in writing with an initial article, "Saying Goodbye to an Old House," published in the *Boston Globe*. This was followed by her columns in the *Middlesex News* (Framingham, MA), and in 1989 she began her "Country Living" column in the *Peterborough Transcript* (Peterborough, NH). In addition, she has served as a contributing writer for the *Portsmouth Herald*, and has written and recorded commentaries for New Hampshire Public Radio. In 1994 she was named Columnist of the Year by the NH Press Association. She is also known throughout New England for her musical programs on poets Emily Dickinson and Celia Thaxter.

Joann Snow Duncanson and her cat, William Wordsworth, live in Peterborough, New Hampshire.